"Everywhere I go women are searching for discipleship tools, either for themselves or for those they are discipling. Katie Orr has delivered up a fresh, substantive tool to accomplish both. FOCUSed15 is a serious study method that is possible even for those with demanding responsibilities. This material will fit in a variety of settings and for women everywhere on their spiritual journey."

—KATHY FERGUSON LITTON, national consultant for
ministry to pastors' wives, North American Mission Board

"Katie Orr brings a unique and productive method of studying Scripture to the world of Bible studies. I enthusiastically encourage women to explore this effective and enjoyable method of Bible study!"

—SUZIE HAWKINS, author and longtime member of
Southern Baptist Convention Pastors' Wives, wife of O. S. Hawkins

"Katie Orr has designed devotional material for the busy woman in mind—a focused 15 minutes a day that leads the reader to encounter the biblical text with guidance that reinforces solid principles of biblical interpretation and helpful application that makes God's Word come alive in our daily choices."

—TREVIN WAX, managing editor of *The Gospel Project*, LifeWay Christian Resources

"Katie Orr has a passion for Scripture and for women to know Scripture. This passion shows in her FOCUSed15 Bible study method, which she uses to lead women through books of the Bible and topical doctrinal studies. She proves that inductive Bible study doesn't have to be complicated but can be deeply impactful and fruitful."

—CHRISTINE HOOVER, author of *From Good to Grace* and *The Church Planting Wife*

"FOCUSed15 gives women an opportunity to learn the tools of inductive Bible study in bite-sized chunks. Perfect for anyone who is committed to studying the Word in this time-crunched culture!"

—ANDREA BUCZYNSKI, vice president of global leadership
development/human resources for CRU

"The Scriptures are like jewels. When you look from different angles they glimmer in beautiful and unexpected ways. FOCUSed15 gives a fresh way to examine and enjoy the most precious words on Earth. Katie Orr's zeal for God's Word is contagious and may forever change the way you engage the Bible."

—JESSE LANE, vice president of connections at Seed Company

"Katie Orr has both the unique ability to make deep, meaningful Bible study doable for others and the passion for helping women love God more through the study of His Word. Through her Bible studies, Katie teaches others how to methodically grasp and absorb biblical theology in digestible bite-sized chunks. Her distinct and approachable gift of leading others through Scripture gives those with a desire to dive into God's Word a wonderful opportunity to both understand and apply deep biblical truths in their everyday."

—CHRYSTAL EVANS HURST, coauthor *of Kingdom Woman*

"I believe weariness is a feeling, and hope is a choice to believe what God says is true really is true. But sometimes, when the storms of life hit, I forget to choose hope, and need someone to come alongside me to help me remember. In this beautiful Bible study, Katie Orr invites us into a deeper understanding of what God's Word has to say about the subject, and reconnects us with the heart of our Savior. There's nothing like diving into Scripture to give a girl hope, and Katie helps us make the leap."

—BROOKE MCGLOTHLIN, president and cofounder of Raising Boys Ministries, and coauthor of *Hope for the Weary Mom: Let God Meet You in the Mess*

EVERYDAY

love

Bearing Witness to
His Purpose

KATIE ORR

Other books in the

FOCUSed15 Bible study series:

Everyday Faith:
Drawing Near to His Presence

Everyday Hope:
Holding Fast to His Promise

FOCUSed
15
Bible
Study

EVERYDAY

love

Bearing Witness to His Purpose

KATIE ORR

NEW HOPE®
PUBLISHERS
Gospel-Centered. Missions-Driven.

BIRMINGHAM, ALABAMA

New Hope® Publishers
PO Box 12065
Birmingham, AL 35202-2065
NewHopePublishers.com
New Hope Publishers is a division of WMU®.

New Hope Publishers serves its authors as they express their views, which may not express the views of the publisher.

Library of Congress Control Number: 2015955249

Cover Designer: Michelle Drashman
Interior Designer: Glynese Northam

ISBN-10: 1-59669-463-7
ISBN-13: 978-1-59669-463-7
N164103 • 0116 • 2M1

Dedication

To my husband: You are a continual example of God-honoring, everyday love. I am honored and thankful I get to be Mrs. Chris Orr. I love you.

Contents

Introduction

We love because he first loved us.

—1 John 4:19

IMAGINE WITH ME: life without media. No TVs, newspapers, or magazines. No smartphones, Internet, or satellites. How would you know what your national leaders look like? What about the latest celebrity or country music star? Would you be able to recognize Oprah if she came to your front door?

In today's culture we have no lack of images. Billboards, pop-up ads, and commercials inundate our days. We are able to see things from all over the world with great detail through various venues. People across the world, even in some of the most remote areas, recognize the Nike swoosh, the red and white Coca-Cola logo, and the blue and white design of Facebook. Commercials send us an image of the product and we recognize their brand because we've seen it over and over again.

In the days before media, national rulers depended on statues in order to be recognized. Without these concrete images the citizens would not know what their sovereign looked like. These figures were set as a declaration, a constant nudge to the people to know who is in charge. In the case of a good king, these statues bred loyalty and drove commitment. It gave people hope and security to know someone was in control and looking out for them.

"So God created man in his own image, in the image of God he created him; male and female he created them" (Genesis 1:27). The original audience of Genesis would have understood the intended meaning of being made in God's image. Images of their own physical ruler would come to mind. They comprehended the great significance of being made in the image of God. You and I are living statues, made in the very image of God. In fact, every soul conceived is made in the image of God. We are reflections, images, and memorials created to bear witness to the glory of our Ruler.

We are His brand and when people see us, they ought to immediately think of our great and glorious God. Mankind was created in God's image, and then two very significant things happened: "And God blessed them. And God said to them, 'Be fruitful and multiply and fill the earth'" (Genesis 1:28).

First, God blessed Adam and Eve. These new image bearers were given the stamp of approval as good and acceptable reflections of His glory, after which came an endorsement. God gave His people a great command: be fruitful and multiply. This charge is not solely speaking to our potential to bear biological children. Included in this command is our God-given purpose to bear witness to the gospel of Jesus Christ, thus bringing forth more displays of the love of God.

We don't have to look far to see that we are broken images that do not reflect the perfect character of our Creator. With the fall of Adam and Eve in the garden (Genesis 2) came a permanent and pervasive defacing of His image bearers. Our sin obstructs an accurate display of God's perfect character. But as we enter into a relationship with God, we are now able to represent the love of Christ to those around us. "Anyone who does not love does not know God, because God is love" (1 John 4:8). This is best done as I obediently listen to the Spirit, obey God's Word, and follow in the footsteps of Jesus to fulfill the charge to "be fruitful and multiply."

We don't have to look far to see we are exhorted—again and again—to love. As we will see through our study of 1 Corinthians 13, love is one of the primary ways we mirror the splendor of Christ to those around us. "Your love for one another will prove to the world that you are my disciples" (John 13:35 NLT). Yet, some of the most unloving people I know are church people. And I'm the first in line. Left to my own way, I choose selfishness instead of love every time. I figure you've picked up this study because you're on a journey of learning to love better, as well. Among other truths, we will see that love is an essential ingredient to every Christian's life, as it is evidence of our Spiritual transformation. So, together, we'll closely examine 1 Corinthians 13 and prayerfully consider God's heart for us when it comes to loving the souls around us.

I'm thrilled you've chosen to take this journey with me.

—Katie

The Need for FOCUS

IF THIS IS your first FOCUSed15 study, you'll want to carefully read through the following introduction and study method instructions. After that, I'll see you on Day 1!

It's hard to focus.

In a world filled with continual demands for my attention, I struggle to keep a train of thought. Tasks I need to do. Appointments I need to remember. Projects I need to complete.

Yeah, it's hard to focus.

Without a good focus for my days, I wander. I lack the ability to choose well and avoid the tyranny of the urgent. Without focus, days become a blur—tossed back and forth between the pressing and the enticing.

WHY FOCUS MATTERS

I felt pretty lost during my first attempts at spending time with God in the Bible. After a few weeks of wandering around the Psalms and flipping through the New Testament, I realized I had no clue what I was doing.

It felt like a pretty big waste of time.

I knew the Bible was full of life-changing truths and life-giving promises, but I needed to learn how to focus on the details to see all that Scripture held for me.

In the medical world, we depend on the microscope. Even with all the fancy machines that can give test results in seconds, the microscope has yet to become obsolete. Some things can only be discovered through the lens of the scope.

What looks like nothing to the naked eye is actually teeming with life-threatening bacteria. Even under the microscope they may not be seen at first glance. But with the smallest adjustment of the focus, the blurry cloud of the field in view is brought into focus and the finest details are revealed.

And those details matter.

You need a microscope to make a diagnosis, but the microscope itself doesn't make the discoveries. It takes a trained eye to distinguish between cells. The average person may be able to figure out how to use the microscope to find a cell and get it in focus, but without training, the beginner will not know the clinical significance of what is seen.

Similarly, when we approach God's Word, we must learn to focus on what we are seeing and develop a trained eye to know its significance.

READY FOR MORE

I grew up in a shallow Christian culture. Don't do drugs. Don't have sex. Don't tell lies. Read your Bible. Be a light—sold-out for Jesus. This was the sum of being a good Christian, or so I thought.

Now, I'm your typical firstborn list-checker, so the do's and don'ts worked for me . . . for a while. But as I got older and the temptations of the don'ts became more enticing, I began to wonder if this Christianity thing was worth it.

Is this really what people spend their lives chasing? Seems tiring—and ultimately worthless.

Yet, God was drawing my heart—I could undeniably feel it—but I knew I was missing something. I thought I'd check out this reading-the-

Bible thing. Sure, I had read a devotional or two and knew all the Bible stories, but I didn't feel I knew God Himself.

A bit nervous, I drove to the local bookstore to buy my first really nice Bible. I excitedly drove back home, and headed straight to my room, opened up my leather-bound beauty and began to read . . .

. . . and nothing happened.

I'm not quite sure what I was expecting, but it sure wasn't confusion and frustration. I decided to give it another try the next day and still heard nothing. I had no clue what I was reading.

In all my years of storing up the do's and don'ts in my how-to-be-a-good-Christian box, I never caught a *how* or *why*.

For years I stumbled through my black leather Bible with very little learned on the other side of it all. Yet, God was faithful to lead and speak, and I fully believe that He can and does speak to us through His Word, even if we are as clueless as I was.

However, I also believe that God's Word is meant to be a great catalyst in our growth, and as we pursue how to better know God through His Word, we will experience Him in deeper ways.

You and I need a healthy, rich diet of God's Word in order to grow. And as we read, study, and learn to digest the Bible, we move toward becoming more like Christ. When we pursue the nearness of God, the don'ts become lackluster compared to the life-giving promises of His Word.

A FOCUSed 15 MINUTES

Over time, I learned incredible Bible study tools that took my time with God in His Word to a deeper level. Yet, with each method, Bible study seemed to take more and more time. Certain seasons of life allow for a leisurely time in the Bible; my experience has proven that most of my days don't.

As much as I would love to find a comfy chair in my favorite local coffee shop and study God's Word for hours, it is just not often possible. I'm lucky if I can get a decent breakfast in every morning before my day starts rolling. Distractions and demands abound, and many days I have not even tried to study my Bible because I just didn't have what it would take, time-wise, to get much out of it.

Until I learned to focus.

Even the busiest Christians can learn to focus and train their eyes to discover the life-changing truths held in Scripture. No incredibly long "quiet times" or seminary degree required.

All it takes is a focused 15 minutes.

The method I will walk you through consists of 15 minutes, five days a week. We will focus on the same set of verses over the course of a week, and each day of that week we will look at the passage with a different lens to gather new insights along the way.

TWO ULTIMATE GOALS

My prayer for you as we dive into the Bible is two-fold. First, I want to work myself out of a job. I want you to walk away from this study a bit more confident in your ability to focus on the transformational truths of Scripture on your own.

Second, I hope you will encounter our God in a deep and meaningful way through these focused 15 minutes. The most important thing about us is what we believe about God, and my prayer is that you will more accurately understand the truths about who He is through your own study of Scripture. As you get to know our glorious God better and better each day, I think you'll see your actions and attitudes are forever changed—because of who He is.

WHAT YOU'LL NEED

A pen to record your study notes and a journal for additional notes and any bonus study work you choose to do.

A Bible. If you don't have one, I recommend investing in a good study Bible. Visit my resources page at KatieOrr.me for solid study Bible suggestions.

Both a Greek interlinear Bible and Greek lexicon. There are in-print and free online versions for both. Check out my resources page for links.

A FEW IMPORTANT NOTES

This is only one method. This approach is my attempt at distilling down how I enjoy spending time in His Word. There are other great methods I use from time to time. Take what you can from this method and use what works for you; make it your own.

Fifteen minutes is just the starting point. Some of us are in a stage of life where we'll take 15 minutes whenever we can get it. Others may be able to carve out more time. I will give you suggestions for how to shorten or lengthen the study as needed. I think you will find yourself looking up at the clock and realizing you've accomplished a lot in a short amount of time.

Using online study tools will be of great help. You can certainly do this study without getting online; however, you will expedite much of the processes through utilizing the powerful—and free—online tools I suggest throughout our time together. I totally get that being online while trying to connect with God has its distracting challenges. Do what works for you. There is no "right" way to do this study. The only way to "fail" is to stop meeting with God.

Resist the urge to consult commentaries and study Bible notes right away. I am thankful for all the resources we have at our fingertips, but oftentimes devotionals, study Bibles, and the latest, greatest Bible teacher can be a crutch that keeps us from learning how to walk intimately with God on our own. While I do believe there is only one true meaning of each verse, God has a personalized word to speak to each of us through this study. Receiving big news from a loved one in a deliberate and personalized way means so much more to us than receiving the news third-hand, and when the Holy Spirit reveals a message to our hearts through God's Word, it will be something we hold to much more closely than someone else's experience of God. If at the end of the week, you are still unsure of the meaning of the passage, you will have time to look through commentaries.

For a list of my favorite online and print resources, including Greek study tools, commentaries, cross-referencing tools, and study Bibles, check out my resources page at KatieOrr.me.

How to FOCUS

OVER THE NEXT four weeks we will study 1 Corinthians 13 together using the FOCUSed15 study method. You may want to think of me as your Bible coach. I will point you to the goal, give you what you need and cheer you on—but you'll be the one doing the work.

The FOCUSed15 method may be different than other studies you've completed. This method is inductive and is great to use verse-by-verse. We're focusing on quality, not quantity. The goal is not to see how quickly we can get through each verse, but how deeply we can go into each verse and find everything we can about God and our role of obedience. Exciting, right?!

The first week we will take a bird's-eye view of the passage, and where it fits in the whole of Scripture. Once we get a handle on the context of this passage, we are going to dive into the text. To do this, I've broken down the passage into three naturally fitting chunks, and we'll spend the remaining three weeks on one section of 1 Corinthians 13. Here is where we are headed:

- Week 1—Overview of 1 Corinthians 13
- Week 2—FOCUSing on 1 Corinthians 13:1–3
- Week 3—FOCUSing on 1 Corinthians 13:4–7
- Week 4—FOCUSing on 1 Corinthians 13:8–13

THE FOCUS METHOD

For me, high school history homework typically consisted of answering a set of questions at the end of the chapter. I quickly found that the best use of my time was to take each question, one at a time, and skim through the chapter with the question in mind. So, if the question was about Constantine, I would read the chapter wearing my "Constantine Glasses." All I looked for were facts about Constantine.

Little did I know then, this "glasses" method would become my favorite way to study God's Word. The FOCUSed15 method is essentially changing to a new pair of glasses with each read, using a different focus than the read before. Together, we will study one passage for five days, each day using a different part of the FOCUS method.

- Day 1—Foundation: Enjoy Every Word
- Day 2—Observation: Look at the Details
- Day 3—Clarification: Uncover the Original Meaning
- Day 4—Utilization: Discover the Connections
- Day 5—Summation: Respond to God's Word

For each day in our study, I list several verses to use this FOCUS study method on. I want you to be able to finish each day's study in 15 minutes, while providing ways to spend more time if you have it. You will have the choice to dive into all of the verses suggested or just one.

FOUNDATION

Enjoy Every Word

Many of us are conditioned to read through Scripture quickly and are often left having no idea what we just read. So, to kick off our studies, we will write out our verses. Nothing too fancy, but an incredibly efficient way to slow down and pay attention to each word on the page.

OBSERVATION

Look at the Details

Truths, promises, and commands are where we practice our daily walk with Christ. The truths of God's Word tell us to what we are supposed to conform our minds. The promises in God's Word are those truths to which we must learn to cling. The commands in God's Word are the guardrails God has given us to help us walk in His presence throughout each day.

For each passage we encounter, we will ask ourselves a set of questions. This set of questions can be applied to any passage. Keep in mind that you might not find the "answer" to each question in every verse you read. These are key questions we are training ourselves to ask each time we sit down to study a passage in Scripture.

TRUTHS—WHAT DOES THIS PASSAGE TEACH ABOUT . . . GOD? . . . LOVE?

Just as we get to know our friends and family a bit better each day, we can also get to know the character of our God better and better over time. As we read and study the Bible, we can view much about what is true of God, cling to the promises of His character, and align our lives to reflect His character to the world around us.

PROMISES—WHAT IS PROMISED TO ME IN THIS PASSAGE?

In many places in Scripture, promises are spelled out for us. Sometimes they are conditional promises: If you do this, then He will do that. Other times they are unconditional promises. These unconditional promises are life giving to a healthy thought-life, resulting in fruitful and joyful day-to-day living. As we learn to see the clear promises in Scripture and believe them to be the glorious truths they are, we can live subject to these truths instead of our wishy-washy emotions.

For example, when feelings of guilt overwhelm, I can hold to the truth that:

- God has removed my sins as far as the east is from the west (Psalm 103:12).
- He no longer counts my sin against me (2 Corinthians 5:19).
- I am a new creation in Christ (2 Corinthians 5:17).
- There is no condemnation for those who are in Christ Jesus (Romans 8:1).

I could go on and on, listing truths throughout the Bible that point to the fact that I am forgiven. As I learn to lean into and hold fast to those truths about what is true of me—because of Christ's work on the Cross—I can combat the lies of the evil one and the deceptiveness of my feelings.

COMMANDS—WHAT CAN I TAKE AWAY FROM THIS PASSAGE AND IMPLEMENT INTO MY LIFE?

- What are the commands given?
- Which characteristics are upheld or rebuked?
- What can I learn from the example of others?

For our study of love, we will center our observation day around searching for truths about love and the characters seen in our passage.

CLARIFICATION

Uncover the Original Meaning

This is going to be fun. We are going to look at the original language of the verses. Our three passages are in the New Testament, so we will be looking up the Greek. To do this we will follow three simple steps:

Step 1: DECIDE which English word to study.

In this step, we will look for any repeated or keywords to look up, then choose one to learn more about.

Step 2: DISCOVER the Greek word in an interlinear Bible.
Next, using an interlinear Bible, we'll find the original Greek word for the word we chose in Step 1.

Step 3: DEFINE the Greek word using a Greek lexicon.
Finally, we will learn about the full meaning of each Greek word using a Greek lexicon, which is very much like a dictionary.

We'll walk through an example together each week. You can also bookmark How to Do a Greek Word Study in the appendix for you to reference throughout the study.

UTILIZATION
Discover the Connections

> The infallible rule of interpretation of Scripture is the Scripture itself: and therefore, when there is a question about the true and full sense of any Scripture . . . it must be searched and known by other places that speak more clearly.
>
> —*The Westminster Confession of Faith*

Ever notice the little numbers and letters inserted in your study Bible? Most have them. The numbers are footnotes, helpful bits of information about the original text. The little letters are cross-references and important tools for study.

Cross-references are doing just that, referencing across the Bible where the word or phrase is used in other passages in the Bible. They may also refer to a historical event or prophecy significant to the verse you are studying.

Together, we will follow a few of the cross-references for each of our passages, as they will often lead us to a better understanding of the main teaching of our verses. If your Bible doesn't have cross-references, no worries! I will provide verses for you to look up, and refer you to online tools for bonus studies.

SUMMATION
Respond to God's Word

> A respectable acquaintance with the opinions of the giants of the past, might have saved many an erratic thinker from wild interpretations and outrageous inferences.
>
> —CHARLES SPURGEON

This is when begin to answer the question "How should this passage affect me?" To do this we will do three things:

1. IDENTIFY—Find the main idea of each passage.
With a robust study of our passage accomplished, we can now do the work of interpretation. Interpretation is simply figuring out what it all means. This is oftentimes difficult to do. However, if we keep in mind the context and make good observations of the text, a solid interpretation will typically result.

This day is when we will finally consult our study Bibles and commentaries! Commentaries are invaluable tools when interpreting Scripture. They are available on the entire Bible, as well as volumes on just one book of the Bible. For a list of free online commentaries, as well as in-print investments, check out KatieOrr.me/Resources.

2. MODIFY—Evaluate my beliefs in light of the main idea.

Once we have figured out what the passage means, we can apply the passage to our lives. Many tend to look at application as simply finding something to change in their actions. Much in the Bible certainly leads us to a different lifestyle, but there is another category of application that we often miss: what we believe.

We must learn to see the character of God in what we study and ask ourselves how our view of Him lines up with what we see. Of course it is helpful to look for do's and don'ts to follow, but without an ever-growing knowledge of who God is, the commands become burdensome.

3. GLORIFY—Align my life to reflect the truth of God's Word.

When we see God for the glorious, grace-filled Savior He is, the natural response is worship; the do's and don'ts become a joy as they become a way to honor the One we love with our lives. Worship is true application.

ALL OF THIS . . . IN 15 MINUTES?!

Yes, I know this seems like a lot of ground to cover. Don't worry! I will be here to walk you through each day. Remember, instead of trying to go as fast as we can through a passage, we are going to take it slow and intentional. We'll study one passage a week, and apply only one part of the method to the passage each day.

THE CHEAT SHEET

At the end of most days' studies, I've included a "cheat sheet." While try-ing to complete a Bible study, I've often been paralyzed with wondering, "Am I doing this the right way?" The cheat sheet is there for you to use as a reference point. It is not a list of correct answers, however, and is meant instead to provide just a little bit of guidance here and there to let you know you are on the right track.

There are also several references in the appendix you may want to refer to throughout our time together. If you are new to Bible study, you might consider spending a day to read through the appendices before beginning your study. I hope those pages will be of great help to you.

A NOTE TO THE OVERWHELMED

Bible study is not a competition or something to achieve. It is a way of communicating with our magnificent God. If you have little time or men-tal capacity (I've been there, moms with little ones!), ignore the bonus study ideas and enjoy what you can. Keep moving through the study each day, and know that you have taken a step of obedience to meet with God in His Word. Other seasons of life will allow for longer, deeper study. For now, embrace these precious moments in the Word and remember that Jesus is your righteousness. When God looks at you—overwhelmed and burned-out though you are—He sees the faithful obedience and perfec-tion of Christ on your behalf, and He is pleased. Rest in that today, weary one.

PREPARING TO **FOCUS**

What Is Biblical Love?

A love letter

PREPARING TO **FOCUS**

MOST OF MY junior high memories involve notes. From the silly cootie catchers (those crazy, folded paper games with hidden messages being the flaps) to the heart-pouring, three-paged declarations of affection, my middle school years were riddled with BFFs, secret clubs, and the dawning of a "love life." I learned many lessons in those years of note writing. One of which I wish I had learned sooner rather than later: the opportunity for misinterpreting a letter is incredibly high.

Written communication has been a part of life for centuries. In fact, many parts of the Bible were originally letters written to a specific audience; they are called epistles. The Book of 1 Corinthians is one of these epistles, a letter from Paul to a church in the city of Corinth.

When studying Scripture, it is always important to figure out the reason behind the writings, especially with these epistles. Since we can't call the authors to ask them what they meant by every word written, we must do a bit of investigative work to figure out the circumstances surrounding the letters. This is a very important step to take before diving into any letter found in the Bible.

To illustrate this in a modern day setting, let's say I sent a text message to my husband that read: "I love AU!" If you happened to see this message, how would you know what AU meant? First, you would need to know who sent the text. It would also be helpful to see the conversation leading up to this text. If the text was sent sometime around July 22 (my birthday), the text could be a not-so-subtle hint to my husband to buy me that gold necklace I've been eyeing, since the symbol for the gold element is "Au." However, AU is also an abbreviation for Australia. If the text was sent around May 10 (our anniversary), we may have just returned home from an amazing trip, and the text was a declaration of how much I loved our time together in the Outback. Another likely meaning for AU could be Auburn University, my alma mater. Since I'm a huge Auburn fan—this would be a good guess, especially if you knew I was at Jordan Hare Stadium, donning my orange and blue getup, and sent immediately after an Auburn touchdown!

Though there are several possible interpretations of my text message, I am the only one who knows without a doubt what "I love AU!" means— because I am the author of the text. But the more you, the reader, understand about when and why it was sent, the more likely your conclusion about the meaning of the message will be accurate.

This is exactly what we need to do first in our study of love. Before we can dive into 1 Corinthians 13, the famous "love chapter," you and I must do the investigative work to better understand the author's original intentions and meaning for the words we will study.

1. Open today's time with a prayer of dedication of the next four weeks. Ask God to guide you as you study and give you grace to practice what you learn from His Word.

2. Read 1 Corinthians 13 three times. With each read, consider using a different translation. I use the English Standard Version for a study like this because it is a great word-for-word translation. I also enjoy reading the New Living Translation for a fresh perspective. Consider reading the passage aloud and/or writing out each verse, depending on what you have time for today.

This is not the time to have all your questions answered, simply become familiar with the verses.

3. As you read, make note of anything that catches your eye, or any questions you have about the text.

My husband and I met in Jacksonville, Florida. To this day, it is one of my favorite places. There are yummy restaurants, eclectic shops, and decadent chocolatiers that boast chocolate-covered popcorn. Yet, it's more than just a fun place. It's where I entered into my calling of full-time ministry, lived a bit of a second college experience, and made lifelong friendships. The River City introduced me to married life and motherhood and it will forever hold a special place in my heart.

Jacksonville is the largest city, by area, in the contiguous United States. At 747 square miles, it took a lot of getting used to before I knew my way around. Slowly but surely, I learned many of the ins and outs of the different areas of the city and even found my own favorite spots, though it took over two years for it to feel like home. Similarly, it takes much time to become acquainted with each book of the Bible. Before we can dive into the details of this passage, we must have a good grip on the big picture of what we are reading. I know you might be ready to dive into the details of everyday love and discover how to be a better image bearer of Christ, but getting a bird's-eye view is a needed and rewarding step towards a better understanding of the truths we will uncover in the weeks to come.

God, I am so thankful for Your Word. It is truly a gift to me.
I'm excited for all that these verses hold for me. Holy Spirit,
continually prepare my heart and mind to accept Your Word
as needed truth.

⁓ BONUS STUDY ⁓

Read 1 Corinthians 1–4. Note anything you learn about the Corinthian church.

Love Is Required

PREPARING TO **FOCUS**

THE APOSTLE PAUL had no biological children, but he had thousands of spiritual offspring, and Paul dedicated His life to the spiritual birth, establishment, and growth of his children, including the church at Corinth. His Corinthian "children" were babies; new in Christ, and messy as can be. Instead of looking to how they could best bear the image of Jesus, they fought over who looked best among them. Their eyes were not on their Savior, rather the Corinthian Christians were competitive, corrupt, and cavalier about their newfound faith. After receiving reports of great immorality and divisions in the church, Paul saw the need to correct and encourage his beloved disciples. Paul wrote to them in hopes of encouraging them to move from their immature state and on toward growth. "But I, brothers, could not address you as spiritual people, but as people of the flesh, as infants in Christ" (1 Corinthians 3:1).

Unfortunately, my actions and attitudes can fall more in line with the immaturity of the Corinthians instead of a clear reflection of Christ's character. We were created as image bearers, remember? We each carry a compelling testimony within us: Our God is the good and gracious giver of eternal life for anyone who would trust in Jesus' perfect life and sufficient sacrifice on the Cross. And if you are in Christ today and hold this study in your hands, it is because God has placed you to be an image bearer to His glory today. He has planted you in your particular time and place to be like a statue, a visible symbol for others around you to see who God is.

Reflecting God's glory and His character becomes clearer to the world when I walk with Jesus. Keeping in step with the Spirit of God brings forth fruit, the kind of fruit that makes people stop and think, "Wow, there is something about her that is different, special." When enabled by the power of God to love people in a supernatural way, I reflect the glory of God to those around me. I have a high and holy calling as an image bearer, and as I press into the presence of God, the natural result of being with Him is an undeniable transformation that others notice. But when I immaturely choose to waste my time and energy chasing after my own pleasures and plans, I am no longer positioned to reflect the light of God to a dark and desperate world.

"Be blameless and innocent, children of God without blemish in the midst of a crooked and twisted generation, among whom you shine as lights in the world" (Philippians 2:15).

1. Open today's time with a prayer of confession. Ask God to reveal the places in your life that are not reflecting His glory to the people around you. Declare your need for God's Spirit to enable you to change.

We're all in progress. We come to Christ a nasty, wretched mess. But He is making all things new, including you and me. He has given us new life and a great hope to look forward to for eternity. As we journey toward the eternal life God has promised us, He is doing a work to make us more and more into the image of His Son. One day we will be like Him in every way. Until then, we are to do all we can to align our lives to reflect the character of Christ. It takes a lot of effort and even more grace, but it is a work He has begun and a work He will complete. Let's hold fast to that truth!

2. Open your Bible to 1 Corinthians 1, and look for any section headings. These headings, just like the chapter and verse numberings, are not original to the biblical manuscripts, but have been added to help organize the abundant, inspired content given to us from the Holy Spirit. For example, in my Bible, the first heading reads: "Divisions in the Church." Looking at these section headings can give a quick and easy way to begin to understand the context for a verse or passage you are studying. (If your Bible doesn't have any headings, check out my resources page for online Bible suggestions. You can also look to the cheat sheet for a list of headings.) Starting with 1 Corinthians 1, working your way through the entire book, write down any section headings that give you insight into the state of the church when Paul penned this letter.

SECTION HEADINGS
Examples: Divisions in the Church (1:10–17)
Divisions in the Church (3:1–18)

3. Just by looking at the clues we have in the headings, what are some of the problems you can see the church was experiencing?

4. What do you think Paul might have hoped the Lord would do through this letter?

The Corinthians struggled. From divisiveness and comparison games to sexual immorality, lawsuits against each other, idolatry, and more. They were a divided, unhealthy church, fumbling around like fish out of water, making a mess of everything around them. Yet Paul did not count them as a lost cause. He never gave up on the power of the gospel in their lives to become beautiful bearers of the good news they've received. There was hope for them, and there is great hope for us, too.

God, I thank You for the people You have put into my life to teach, mold, and correct my sinful ways. I praise You for the hope we have in the gospel, that once we are in Christ there is nothing we can do that can separate us from His love. I open up my heart for You to work in deeper ways in my life.

⁘ BONUS STUDY ⁘

Look up the introductory sections your study Bible (or an online study tool) has about the 1 Corinthians epistle.

Read 1 Corinthians 5–8. Note anything you learn about the Corinthian church.

CHEAT SHEET

2. Section headings in 1 Corinthians. These headings will vary, depending on which study Bible or online resource you are using. Here are the headings that stood out to me. (Quoted from my *ESV Study Bible*.) You may have written others down, and that is fine. My hope is that you get a glimpse of all Paul was writing about, and the state of the church at the time. Immorality, idolatry, division, and dissension seem to be pervasive among the church people of Corinth.

SECTION HEADINGS
Sexual Immorality Defiles the Church (5:1–13)
Lawsuits Against Believers (6:1–11)
Flee Sexual Immorality (6:12–20)
Warning Against Idolatry (10:1–22)
Do All to the Glory of God (10:23–33)
One Body with Many Members (12:12–31)
The Way of Love (13:1–13)
Orderly Worship (14:26–40)

Love, Above All

PREPARING TO **FOCUS**

For from him and through him and to him are all things. To him be glory forever. Amen.

—ROMANS 11:36

MULTITASKING COMES NATURALLY for me. In fact, I am much more productive when my schedule is full and my days are busy. With this ability comes great benefits at times, but it can also cause disorder and distraction when I need to focus in on one thing. If I set out to get a certain project done around the house, staying on task is a struggle. Countless loads of laundry have been forgotten in the washer because I try to sneak it in as a side note to my day, instead of approaching the baskets with a decent plan. Drawers or closets that need purging and organizing get just enough attention to make the room look like a disaster area before I'm off to tackle something else. Some of this is due to my stage of life, with three young children and all their needs and demands, but much of it is due to my own lack of being able to complete a task from start to finish.

Distraction from the end goal comes easy. For me, this diversion doesn't end with housework. I continually find myself off course in my efforts to follow Jesus. The original plan may have been to serve and honor Him, but I inevitably end up pursuing my own glory and satisfaction, and as a divided image bearer, I do not accurately reflect the purpose of the One who sent me.

Yesterday we learned one reason Paul wrote this letter was to correct the Corinthians. Secondarily, Paul also responded to a set of questions the church had previously sent him. After Paul addressed their lack of unity, lack of discipline, and lack of purity, he answered some of these questions. "Now concerning matters about which you wrote . . ." (1 Corinthians 7:1). However, they didn't send him questions like, "Will you please tell us how to better glorify God with our everyday?" or, "Paul, how do we love each other better?" No, their questions were self-centered, and revealed their desire to be recognized and elevated among others. This chapter of love we are getting ready to dive into is smack dab in the middle of Paul's answer to one of their questions.

Though the verses in 1 Corinthians 13 are familiar and beautiful, now often displayed on coffee mugs and framed art, we sometimes mistakenly assign their meaning primarily to romantic relationships. While the teachings held in 1 Corinthians 13 certainly have implications for marriage, Paul's original intention in writing was not specifically directed toward couples. It was directed as a rebuke to the church and holds significance for every relationship found within the body of Christ.

Like me, the Corinthians were distracted. They may have originally set out to bear witness of the Christ they came to know, but somewhere along the way they derailed. Their focus shifted from sacrificially giving to self-centered receiving. Their goals morphed into a craving for personal accolades and cultural significance, ignoring the Source of the gifts they were endowed. Their desire to be noticed and praised trumped the calling to steward their God-given abilities.

Instead of following in the footsteps of the Corinthians, we can all learn from the attitude of King David seen in his prayer of dedication. During a monumental celebration, Israel brought their abundant offerings to build a temple for God. Overwhelmed by the goodness of God,

David declares: "But who am I, and what is my people, that
we should be able thus to offer willingly? For all things come from you"
(1 Chronicles 29:14).

1. Ask God to focus your heart onto primary things today and to reveal any
sources that cause distraction from your heart's purpose to bear witness to
Jesus.

2. Read 1 Corinthians 12:1–14:25. This is the answer Paul gives for one of the
questions he received. What do you think the Corinthian church's question
was concerning?

3. Write out 1 Corinthians 12:31 below:

4. What do you think the main point of 1 Corinthians 12:31 is?

5. Write out 1 Corinthians 14:1 below:

6. What do you think the main point of 1 Corinthians 14:1 is?

7. How does seeing this book of love in its context change what you thought about these verses?

One of the self-centered questions the Corinthians sent Paul was about spiritual gifts. Specifically, they wanted to know which ones were to be regarded as highest. First Corinthians 12:1–14:25 is Paul's answer to that particular question. In chapter 12 we find the great teaching on how believers are "one body, many parts." We are to be unified in our diversity and value each other's strengths, which supplement our own weaknesses. Paul ended chapter 12 with, "But earnestly desire the higher gifts. And I will show you a still more excellent way" (v. 30). Fast-forward to

14:1. Paul commanded them to "pursue love, and earnestly desire the spiritual gifts." He told them that their desire for spiritual gifts was good, but they were missing the point. They had things out of order.

Tucked between these two truths is a great teaching on this "most excellent way"—living a life of biblical love. We must view these verses as the meat of a sandwich; the main dish in a dinner of understanding how to be unified in our differences. So when dissensions stem from comparison, and distractions arise from self-centered living, we know that we have missed the main point. And that main point is always God's glory, not ours.

> Yours, O LORD, is the greatness and the power and the glory and the victory and the majesty, for all that is in the heavens and in the earth is yours. Yours is the kingdom, O LORD, and you are exalted as head above all. Both riches and honor come from you, and you rule over all. In your hand are power and might, and in your hand it is to make great and to give strength to all. And now we thank you, our God, and praise your glorious name.
>
> —1 CHRONICLES 29:11–13

⁙ BONUS STUDY ⁙

Read 1 Corinthians 9–12. Note anything you learn about the Corinthian church.

Love Is Expected

PREPARING TO **FOCUS**

He is like a tree planted by streams of water that yields its fruit in its season, and its leaf does not wither. In all that he does, he prospers.

—Psalm 1:3

BABIES ARE SUCH . . . babies. It's pretty amazing how these tiny beings can bring an incredible amount of joy to life when all they do is sleep, cry, eat, and produce dirty diapers. Yet each of these not-always-so-pleasant activities is a sign of vitality and growth in a newborn. We expect babies to act like babies and when they don't, we begin to wonder if something is amiss. In fact, doctors and midwives pay very close attention to these newborn activities in the early months after birth. The absence of crying, a failure to feed, or problems eliminating are all red flags of a deeper problem.

We expect a baby to grow, and the same is true with fruit trees. A healthy, thriving apple tree will put out shoots, branches, leaves, and eventually produce the fruit it was planted for. If you plant, feed, prune, and water the trees, yet it never produces apples, there is a problem somewhere. A lack of fruit should bring forth questions about the vitality of the tree.

Just as certain rhythms are expected from a newborn, and it is right to anticipate fruit from a thriving apple tree, there are also undeniable signs of spiritual life that are natural results of a person who belongs

47

Christ. One of the greatest signs of life in a regenerate believer (one who is transformed by the power of the gospel of Christ) is, you guessed it, love. If love is lacking, something is ailing.

1. Circle the words below which best describe your life as of late.

thriving   fruitless   fruitful   withering   firmly planted

healthy   unhealthy   full of life   apathetic   lifeless

2. Spend a few moments in contemplative prayer, and ask the Holy Spirit to gently reveal to you places in your life that do not show signs of spiritual vitality. Confess those places of needed change. Thank God for His forgiveness, and ask Him for the strength to draw near to His transforming presence.

3. We are going to look at John 13:34–35 today, but before you read those words, take a peek at the headings in John 12 and 13 and write out any events that have taken place. If you have extra time today, feel free to read through the chapter to get a deeper look at each event. (Remember, if your Bible doesn't have section headings, most of the free online and mobile app Bibles have them.)

Example: Jesus is anointed by Mary (12:1–8)

4. Now read John 13:34–35. This is an account of one conversation during what is famously known as the Last Supper. Jesus is hours away from being betrayed, arrested, beaten, and crucified, and this is His last chance to encourage and equip His nearest disciples and dearest friends before His death. What command does Jesus give His dear disciples in John 13:34–35?

Jesus spent three long years carefully pouring into these men, and this account is from the last day He has with them, when He uncovers a new commandment: love. To this group of men who desire to follow Jesus with all they have, and immediately after Judas Iscariot leaves the group to betray the Son of God, He exhorts them to love one another. In that moment of incredible intimacy with Jesus, I'm sure they never dreamed how difficult that command would be to fulfill.

5. Look up 1 John 4:21. Note below what commandment we have from God.

6. Spend some time evaluating the presence or absence of love in your life. Journal through the following questions:

Is there evidence of a growing love for others in my life?

Is my spiritual growth stunted, even nonexistent? Why might that be?

Though the command to love is a difficult one to follow, it is nonetheless expected. If you are a Christian, you love. Conversely, if your life is not characterized by a supernatural love for others, then the gospel of Jesus has not penetrated your life. The expected result of a person who knows Jesus intimately is a life filled with sacrificial love.

> *As the Father has loved me, so have I loved you. Abide in my love. If you keep my commandments, you will abide in my love, just as I have kept my Father's commandments and abide in his love. These things I have spoken to you, that my joy may be in you, and that your joy may be full.*
>
> —JOHN 15:9–11

> *God, the command to love is incredibly daunting. My heart is willing, but my flesh is weak. I set out each day to do better, love greater, yet I stumble again and again on this path of*

love. Holy Spirit, rise up into every part of my heart; bring Your awakening to my weakness, Your power to my deficiency.

⁂ BONUS STUDY ⁂

Read 1 Corinthians 13–16. Note anything you learn about the Corinthian church.

CHEAT SHEET

3. We are going to look at John 13:34–35 today, but before you read these words, take a peek at the headings in John 12 and 13 and write out any events that have taken place. If you have extra time today, feel free to read through the chapter to get a deeper look at the events.

• Jesus is anointed by Mary (12:1–8)

• There is a plot to kill Lazarus (12:9–11)

• Jesus enters Jerusalem/Palm Sunday (12:12–19)

• Jesus speaks about eternal life, foretells His departure (12:20–50)

• Last Supper/Jesus washes disciples' feet (13:1–20)

• Jesus foretells Judas's betrayal (13:21–30)

• Jesus begins final instructions to His disciples (13:31–35)

4. Read John 13:34–35, an account of the last supper. What command does Jesus give in John 13:34–35?

• Love one another, as I have loved you

5. Look up 1 John 4:21. Note below what commandment we have from God.

• Whoever loves God must also love his brother.

Love Is Evidence

PREPARING TO FOCUS

Anyone who does not love does not know God, because God is love.

—1 John 4:8

LOVE IS AN expectation for every Christian. However, if it is expected, why isn't love more evident in the lives of His people? I'm a people bulldozer without Jesus. Most people annoy me, and left to my fleshly desires I would rather be left alone to work through my checklist than have to stop and do things for other people. Serving others is not a naturally enjoyable event for me, and I certainly don't like giving others what they want if it affects my comfort. I continually struggle to love others over myself, because my selfish heart craves my own way, in my own timing, on my own terms. I'm an arrogant, selfish being.

As sad as this reality is, it gives me great hope and confidence in my salvation because I have seen evidence of biblical love in my life. Love displayed in my everyday is nothing short of a miraculous work of the Holy Spirit in my life. If my family feels served, blessed, and loved by me, it is supernatural fruit of the Holy Spirit's empowering presence within me.

A genuine love for others bears witness to the fact that I am greatly loved by a gracious God—and this true love for others cannot be faked. This ability to love others with a biblical love is only evidenced in those who have experienced a regenerating work of God. If you spend your days uncertain of your position in Christ, may I encourage you to look for the evidence of Christ-like love in your life? Not the kind of love that can be conjured up on your own, but the kind that you look back and say, "Where did that come from?" If you find it hard to find evidence of godly love in your life, consider two common causes.

I do not love because I have not experienced and accepted the love of God.

A lack of love for others could point to the fact that you've never truly experienced the life change that occurs through Christ. You and I are sinners. This sin nature separates us from God, who is holy and just and must punish wrongdoing—just as any righteous judge would. But God, because He loves us so much, put into motion a drastic rescue plan. He sent us His son, Jesus. Through the perfect life of Christ, a holy sacrifice needed to pay the penalty of sin's demand was provided. By His sacrifice on the Cross, Jesus provided the miracle we all need—a way for the wretched soul to stand righteous before God. However, you may be able to know about this good news and acknowledge its truth without truly experiencing it. You can ascribe to the doctrine of grace, but not depend on it. You can know all about God, but not actually know Him personally.

This spiritual transformation only occurs through faith. It is not enough to know about this work of Christ on the Cross, you must draw near to our holy God with a confidence that Jesus' provision on your behalf is enough, then hold fast to His provision of righteousness as your only hope. This is the gospel, the good news that we can enter into a personal relationship with God by faith alone. If you have never admitted your need for all Christ has done for you, and chosen to follow His path for your life as an act of worship, I encourage you to look through the explanation of the gospel in the appendix, and find a leader or friend who can discuss it and pray with you.

I do not love because I have forgotten the love of God.

A second reason for lovelessness to consider: you are forgetful. You have accepted the gospel of Christ and experienced initial life change, but you have drifted away from clinging to Christ in your everyday. When we truly come to understand all God has provided for us through Christ, we see everything and everyone through the glasses of His grace. Our love-lessness is often evidence of our forgetfulness.

> The gospel is not merely the diving board off of which we jump into the pool of Christianity, it's also the pool itself.
>
> —J. D. GREEAR

1. Open today's study time in prayer. Ask God to open your eyes to the transforming truths in His Word.

2. Look back at yesterday's passage, John 13:34–35. What does Jesus say is the natural evidence of being a disciple of Christ?

3. Now, read 1 John 4:7–8 and list out all that is true about love.

4. Read also 1 John 3:14 and note what you learn about love.

The good news of Jesus is not reserved for Vacation Bible School and revival services. It isn't a one-time, down-the-aisle experience. It's a lifeline, a day-to-day essential. We cannot go from death to life without the power of the gospel. Neither can we, without the power of the gospel,

go from being a person marked by hate to becoming someone who chooses everyday love. Love is an outward proof of an internal
transformation. Genuine, sacrificial, godly love cannot happen without a
complete heart change and a continual dependence on the Spirit of God
to bring about the fruit of that change into our daily lives. (For additional
study on the gospel and how it transforms our daily lives, I encourage
you to check out my _Everyday Hope_ Bible study.)

"By this all people will know that you are my disciples, if you have
love for one another" (John 13:35).

> _God, forgive me for my forgetfulness of how desperate I am_
> _for Your grace. Help me in my moments of lovelessness not_
> _to give in to guilt or despair but to draw near to You in faith_
> _that the power of Your gospel can and will bring forth love in_
> _my life, as I learn to depend on Your grace._

⋅ː⋅ BONUS STUDY ⋅ː⋅

Take additional time to summarize what you learned each day of this
week and journal through the following questions:

1. Stop a moment to think back on your life. Can you with certainty look back
to a time where the eyes of your heart were enlightened to the reality of your
sin and your desperate need for the righteousness of Christ? Write down a bit
about your salvation experience.

2. Now think through your life since that point of salvation. Is there evidence in your day-to-day living that points back to the work of Christ in your heart?

3. Are you experiencing the power of the gospel in your everyday life?

4. What is God leading you to do as a result of this week's study?

CHEAT SHEET

2. What does Jesus say is the natural evidence of being a disciple of Christ?
Love for one another

3. Read 1 John 4:7–8 and list out all you learn about love.

• The Christian is to love others.

• Love is from God.

• Anyone who has the ability to love has been born of God and truly knows
  God.

• Anyone who does not love does not know God.

• God is love.

4. Read also 1 John 3:14 and note what you learn about love.

• We can know that we have passed out of death into life through the evidence of love in our life.

• Whoever does not love remains in death.

FOCUSING ON **1 CORINTHIANS 13:1–3**

Love Is Essential

Foundation

FOCUSing ON 1 CORINTHIANS 13:1–3

MY VOLLEYBALL COACH called it the bag of wonders. I took it on every away game road trip, and this pink satchel contained everything a tween girl could need. Essentially, I carried around a "mom bag" before I knew such a thing existed. You know the one: the gigantic, overloaded bag with random items "just in case." The good Girl Scout in me has a need to always be prepared. (In other words, I have hoarding tendencies.)

The definition of what I truly need has changed over time. These days, I carry my essentials in an iPhone case that boasts a card slot on the back. Just enough for the essentials: my debit card, credit card, and drivers license. I can even throw a $10 bill in there. All I need are my keys and my phone. That's it. No more gigantic bag of wonders. However, if I ever lose my phone I'm in big trouble.

The Bible exhorts us over and over to love. Love is essential to the Christian life and (as we'll see in this week's passage) if we forsake love, we miss something essential. We like to make Christian living about many nonessentials. I call them the do's and don'ts. We get wrapped up with our checklists and appearances and, when we do, we turn walking with Christ into a performance for others or a goal to achieve and we miss the abundant life Christ died for us to experience. We carry around our own spiritual bag of wonders, filled with all our Christian moralism, activities, and spiritual makeup hoping to fool others into thinking we've got it all together. All the while, we've forgotten the true essentials at home.

This week, we get to dive into the FOCUSed15 study method. If this is your first FOCUSed15 study, you might want to go back and read through the explanation again, and bookmark that page for easy reference. We'll be walking through it together, not only to learn about love in 1 Corinthians 13, but also to provide you with a structure you can walk through other passages on your own.

1. Open your time in the Word with a prayer of thankfulness for the love God has poured out on you. Journal your prayer below.

ENJOY EVERY WORD

2. Today, we'll work through our first layer of studying 1 Corinthians 13:1–3 by writing the passage. You can write the verse out word-for-word, diagram the sentences (like in fourth grade English class!), or even draw the passage with images that communicate each verse. Do whatever helps you slow down and enjoy what is communicated in these verses. There is no right or wrong way to do this. It is simply an exercise of intentionally taking in each word.

We'll build on what we learn from this practice throughout the rest of the week.

3. What stands out to you in 1 Corinthians 13:1–3? What questions do you have about the passage?

Intentionality and preparedness go a long way when it comes to sticking with the essentials of life. Whether it's what I carry in my pocket or carry in my heart, I have choices to make if I want to keep the main thing the main thing. Love is essential to life, but I must be intentional to keep it in its rightful place in my life. If I want to love better, I must walk with God because love is an essential, natural overflow of being with Jesus.

> *God, help me to recognize when I am acting out of something other than love. I confess I am all too easily distracted by my checklist and aspirations. I forget to make loving You and loving others an essential in my everyday. By Your grace, I will choose better today.*

⊱ BONUS STUDY ⊰

Work toward memorizing 1 Corinthians 13:1–3. Write out these verses on a few notecards and post them around your house. Take some time to find a memorization app for your phone and upload these verses. (I have app recommendations on my resources page.)

Observation

FOCUSing ON 1 CORINTHIANS 13:1–3

If I speak in the tongues of men and of angels, but have not love, I am a noisy gong or a clanging cymbal.

—1 Corinthians 13:1

THERE IS AN old home VHS video of my sister, Sarah, sitting at the kitchen table moping. This particular evening, seven-year-old Sarah was not happy with the menu, and a plate full of meatloaf lay at the table in front of her. My parents held us to the rule that we had to eat what was prepared for us before we could get up from the table. So Sarah sat, arms crossed, pouting. My dad held the 1980s camcorder to get a view of the sight while he interviewed my sister about the situation. Her answers to his questions about dinner were not pleasant, and Daddy's peppy advice to her was: "Sarah, don't let your meatloaf loaf!" Needless to say, she was not enjoying his humor.

My dad took an interesting approach to many common parenting issues. A jokester at heart, he would try to infuse laughter into less than ideal situations. When I would whine, "I'm hungry!" my dad would respond, with his hand outstretched to shake mine, "Hi, Hungry! I'm Jim." and proceed to shake the life out of my arm. The incessant shaking was annoying enough that I learned to think twice before stating my dissatisfaction with life through whining. Whining is an ineffective tactic in most households, just as it was in my childhood home. Though my own kids have heard "I don't listen to whining" 100 times, they continually insist on utilizing that high-pitched tone of voice. (Maybe I need to revert to a few of my father's fun parenting tactics!)

Today, we continue our study of 1 Corinthians 13:1–3. Paul is carrying on his point from chapter 12. Remember, all of chapters 12–14 answer the Corinthians' question, "Which spiritual gift is best, Paul?" He likens the people of God to each being one of many parts of the body. Every piece is essential to the body, regardless of its purpose. And just like you can't have a properly functioning body with missing parts, every spiritual gift given to God's people is a needed one. Not only that, but there is no gift that is greater than others. However, Paul does say there is a "more excellent way" than fighting over the use of spiritual gifts, and he explains this way of love and how our effectiveness as Christians is made possible by the role love plays.

When we live life without love, we are like a child's moaning and groaning attempts at requesting a pass on meatloaf—filled with ineffective noise. At the core of whining is selfishness. I want what I want when I want it. And when my "needs" are not being met, I'm going to let everyone know about it. Unfortunately, many of us use our gifts— the very abilities God has given us to bear witness to Him—for our own pleasure and glory. When we utilize our natural abilities for our own gain, our usual response when things do not go our way is to have a temper tantrum. For some, it may all be internal, but in some shape or form, we behave like a disappointed child who isn't getting her way. Yet defiance gets us nowhere, and the previous "service" for God is simply useless noise in the kingdom of God.

1. Open your time with a prayer of petition, asking God to shape your definition of love to reflect the biblical teaching of love we are learning about.

LOOK AT THE DETAILS

2. Read 1 Corinthians 13:1–3, looking for truths about love, and the implications of acting without love. Record your findings in the chart below. I've filled out the first one for you.

ACTIONS MADE	WITHOUT LOVE	IMPLICATIONS OF LOVELESSNESS
Example: if I speak in the tongues of men and of angels	but have not love	I am a noisy gong or a clanging symbol

3. Which of these implications about lovelessness stands out to you?

Without love, I am noise. Ineffective. Useless. I can do "great" things for God, but if it is not out of an overflow of love for Him and His people—as useful and intentional as I may try to be—I am more like a grumbling, selfish child than an effective minister of the gospel.

God, open my eyes to the places where I am acting out of something other than love. Show me where I am simply longing to be useful and helpful to others, so that they would praise me, instead of acting out of a love for You and that person. Open my eyes to the greed, selfishness, self-righteousness, and other potential pitfalls that keep me from loving others more than myself. Grant me your grace to change my ways.

⋅!⋅ BONUS STUDY ⋅!⋅

Read the following passages and note what you learn about the connection between the body of Christ and spiritual gifts.

Romans 12:3–8

Ephesians 4:11–13

CHEAT SHEET

2. Read 1 Corinthians 13:1–3, looking for truths about love, and the implications of acting without love. Record your findings in the chart below.

ACTIONS MADE	WITHOUT LOVE	IMPLICATIONS OF LOVELESSNESS
speak in tongues	but have not love	I am noise
• prophetic powers • understand all mysteries • understand all knowledge • have all faith, even move mountains	but have not love	I am nothing
• give away everything • sacrifice my body to be burned	but have not love	I gain nothing

Clarification

FOCUSing ON 1 CORINTHIANS 13:1–3

I LIKE TO work out, but I'm not much of a self-propeller when it comes to exercising on my own. I tend to whimp out and give up way too early. That's why I love gym classes. There is always someone to catch up to, and that gives me just the right amount of competitiveness to get myself into gear. There is one class in particular that has become my favorite, though I never would have guessed it would be: running class.

I am not a natural runner. I hated conditioning day in high school volleyball practice. Hated it. When I run I get all red-faced and my lungs do this thing where they gasp for air and scream at my brain to "Just stop already!" When I first starting working out regularly, I couldn't complete half a mile without stopping. But over time, I began to see the tiniest bit of endurance build up. That half-mile route became routine, then after more time, it became my warm up. To date, my record is four miles, a distance I truly thought out of reach. There is great power in showing up and simply trying. What once seemed difficult and daunting has become, dare I say, easy and enjoyable.

You might have peeked ahead at today's study and saw the word *Greek* and kind of cringed inside. It's OK, you can admit it. (I won't tell anyone.) Maybe the hesitation I feel as a beginner runner is similar to what you feel when it comes to Greek study? May I encourage you to simply show up and try it out? I think you too might one day find it easy and enjoyable.

1. Open today's time with prayer, thanking God for the depths of His living and active Word and the tools needed to dive into it.

UNCOVER THE ORIGINAL MEANING

Studying the Greek can be as simple as looking up a word in the dictionary with the right tools. If this is your first attempt at Greek study, I encourage you to check out the videos I've created to show you how to use many of the online Greek tools. Just head to KatieOrr.me/Resources and look for the videos section.

Step 1: DECIDE which English word you would like to study.
To start your Greek study, look for any potential keywords in 1 Corinthians 13:1–3. As you find any repeated word or words that seem important to the passage, write them down below. Maybe you have the word *love* on your list? Let's study this word together.

Step 2: DISCOVER the Greek word in an interlinear Bible.
Now that you know what you want to study, you can look up the English word *love* in an interlinear Bible to find out what the original Greek word is. An interlinear Bible will show you English verses and line up each word next to the Greek words they were translated from.

Let's take the first phrase of 1 Corinthians 13:1 to see how this works: "If I speak in the tongues of men and of angels, but have not love . . ."

In Greek, it looks like this: "ἐὰν ταῖς γλώσσαις τῶν ἀνθρώπων λαλῶ καὶ τῶν ἀγγέλων ἀγάπην δὲ μὴ ἔχω . . ." (GNT Morph).

Most people (including me!) can't read this, so the transliteration of the Greek is often provided for us as well. This transliteration is the Greek words turned into words that use English letters to spell out how the Greek is read. For example, the first Greek words we see, "ἐὰν" and "ταῖς," are transliterated into "ean" and "ho," which is how they are pronounced.

The interlinear Bible simply lines up the two versions (and usually the transliteration as well) so we can see which word goes with which, like this:

ἐὰν	ταῖς	γλώσσαις	τῶν'	ἀνθρώπων	λαλῶ	καὶ
ean	ho	glōssa	ho	anthrōpos	laleō	kai
if	the	tongues	of	men	I speak	and

τῶν	ἀγγέλων	ἀγάπην	δὲ	μὴ	ἔχω
ho	aggelos	agape	de	mē	echō
of	angels	love	but	not	have

You can use this layout to find the original word for *love*. Do you see it?
love = agape = ἀγάπην

Step 3: DEFINE that Greek word using a Greek lexicon.
Now that you know the original word for *love* used in 1 Corinthians 13:1–3 is *agape*, you can look up that Greek word in a Greek lexicon (which is like a dictionary) and note the following:

Lexicon discovery: agapē
- Definition: love
- Times used: 117
- Part of speech: noun

- Other ways it is translated: charity, dear, charitably
- Any special notes: Strong's Greek #26; "it is a love with deep respect (1 Peter 2:17) . . . Unlike other loves, which can remain hidden in the heart, it is essential to charity to manifest itself, to demonstrate itself, to provide proofs, to put itself on display; so much so that in the NT it would almost always be necessary to translate agapē as 'demonstration of love.'"

Pretty simple, right?

Now, why don't you try it on your own? Look up the word *give* in verse 3.

Give =

Lexicon discovery:

• Definition:

• Times used:

• Part of speech:

• Other ways it is translated:

• Any special notes:

If this Greek work is too overwhelming, consider simply looking up a few words in the dictionary and write down what you learn about each word.

2. What discoveries did you make through your clarification study?

God has created me to be a teacher, and in many ways I feel His delight when I am guiding others to truth. However, I like to be looked up to and I can easily find my significance in others learning from me. If I am not careful, my efforts to live out God's call on my life to help others in their walk with Him can turn into me striving to find my place amidst a platform of leaders. When I "serve" out of a desire to be significant and influential, I do the exact opposite of what I was created to do. Yet, when I work out of a love for others, and an overflow of my love for God, I become significant in the kingdom work of God as He chooses to use my lame attempts at ministry for His glory.

We're all seeking significance. It can be in our status among peers and colleagues, or our service to friends and family. Only the work done in love will add toward kingdom significance. Popularity and big numbers don't catch God's eye; He isn't searching for the most talented or busiest. Through Christ, we already have great significance in God's eyes, and when we start from an overflow of security in who God has made us and complete our work as simply an offering of love to Him, it is then that we can walk with a sense of kingdom worth.

I can boast divine inspiration, deep knowledge, and a skilled discernment, but I am nothing without love. "And if I have . . . but have not love, I am nothing" (1 Corinthians 13:2).

God, I am so thankful that my significance is not tied to my performance. Continue to reveal to me the places where I am clinging to my actions and achievements to find worth.

⁙ BONUS STUDY ⁙

Look up additional words throughout each verse in this week's passage.

Step 1: DECIDE which English word you would like to study.

Step 2: DISCOVER the Greek word in an interlinear Bible.

Step 3: DEFINE that Greek word using a Greek lexicon.

Look up that Greek word in a Greek lexicon (which is like a dictionary) and note the following:

Lexicon discovery:
• Definition:
• Times used:
• Part of speech:
• Other ways it is translated:
• Any special notes:

CHEAT SHEET

Step 3: DEFINE that Greek word using a Greek lexicon.

Give = psōmisō

Lexicon discovery: psōmisō

• Definition: feed

• Times used: 2

• Part of speech: verb

• Other ways it is translated:

• Any special notes: Strong's #5595; other occurrence in Romans 12:20 "if your enemy is hungry feed him"; This is most likely a reference to mercy ministry, and sacrificing all you have for the sake of those in need. We can be the biggest philanthropist, but not have love, and it mean nothing in God's economy.

Utilization

FOCUSing ON 1 CORINTHIANS 13:1–3

If I give away all I have, and if I deliver up my body to be burned, but have not love, I gain nothing.

—1 Corinthians 13:3

OUR CULTURE IS obsessed with getting what we deserve. Just about every commercial out there is centered on rewarding ourselves, and I buy into it all the time. When I go out of my way for someone, I want recognition of my efforts, a reward of words. When I go above and beyond at work, a bonus at the end of the year is a welcomed accolade. And when I get through a hard exercise class, I get to reward myself with a big bowl of mint chocolate chip ice cream. (I really need to break this one!)

Not surprisingly, my kids are like proverbial apples—they don't fall far from the tree. Oftentimes, after a good solid session of work from my children to clean the house, my kids will ask, "Mom, what do I get for cleaning my room?" They desire to be rewarded for every good and helpful task they do. They forget they are taken care of in every basic way, and then some. When we are at the grocery store, they sometimes get to pick out a treat from the candy aisle. They regularly receive little gifts from Mom and Dad, just because, plus the typical birthday and Christmas gifts. They receive love, attention, and gifts because they are Orr children, but they also have responsibilities because they are part of that same Orr family. So, when the question arises about what reward they will receive for the work they are doing—work that is expected as being part of the family—the answer is always the same: they've already received their reward. (They don't always like this answer.) When we go on vacation as a family, or we buy them school supplies and another pair of shoes, it's all a benefit of being part of the Orr family.

Every soul has that same desire to be rewarded for every action. But as long as we hold onto this entitlement—the desire for an instant reward—we lose sight of why we're here. You and I do not exist to be rewarded on this earth. We have already been greatly rewarded through Christ as a result of now being part of the family of God, and there are many more rewards to come. Instead of desiring temporary, earthly rewards, we must remember we are sojourners, on the path toward our heavenly home where true and lasting rewards await. (For a deeper study on life as a sojourner, check out one of my other FOCUSed15 Bible studies, *Everyday Faith*.)

1. Open up today's time with God through a prayer of enlightenment. Ask God to guide you as you flip through the pages of His Word today.

DISCOVER THE CONNECTIONS

2. Read 1 Corinthians 13:1–3 to start your study. Look up each reference below, and take notes from any passages that reveal a bigger picture of the threads this verse is attached to. Record what you learn below. You might consider applying one or more of the FOCUS method steps to this passage, depending on the time you have today. I typically enjoy listing out truths I see, especially those that help me understand the original passage I'm studying. You can write out the passage in the space provided, or even look up a word or two in your interlinear Bible. Just do what interests you and what you have time for.

13:2—"prophetic powers"
Matthew 7:22–23

13:3—"If I give away all I have"
Matthew 6:1–4

Earthly rewards are gone in an instant, while heavenly rewards are enjoyed for eternity. Clinging to an eternal perspective—remembering why I exist and where I am heading—changes everything.

God, help me to see every moment through the lens of eternity. Enable me, Holy Spirit, to choose well. Help me to look forward to the rewards of heaven more than the instant gratification of the things I see in front of me.

∴ BONUS STUDY ∴

Look up the cross-references for additional phrases in this week's passage. Continue on until you need to move on with your day. If your Bible does not have cross-references in it, check out the online cross-references recommendations at KatieOrr.me/Resources.

You could easily spend two or three days, 15 minutes or more at a time, working through each verse. Remember, these days are simply suggestions. Follow God's leading. If He tells you to slow down and dig deep, go for it!

CHEAT SHEET

2. Read 1 Corinthians 13:1–3 to start your study. Look up each reference below, and take notes from any passages that reveal a bigger picture of the threads this verse is attached to. Record what you learn below.

13:2—"prophetic powers"

Matthew 7:22–23

There will be many who prophesied and did "many mighty works" in the name of God, but He will say He never knew them.

13:3—"If I give away all I have"

Matthew 6:1–4

Work done for the praise of others will be rewarded when the praise from others is received. Work done out of love will receive an eternal reward, which comes from God. Christ warns that if we give only to be seen by others, we receive our reward then and there. Our reward is the approval of man, therefore there is no eternal reward. This is why Paul says, "I gain nothing."

Summation

FOCUSing ON 1 CORINTHIANS 13:1–3

I LOVE CONFERENCES. I'm your typical extrovert who loves being surrounded by new people to learn more about and old friends to connect with. In these retreat settings, I am typically consumed with the conversation at hand, and it's easy to lose track of time or forget basic tasks. On more than one occasion, I've piled into the elevator while in conversation with a group of friends. The dialogue continues until the elevator door opens up on the same floor we originated, and we realize no one pushed the elevator button!

If you get on an elevator, even with the best of intentions to make it to the tenth floor, you won't get very far if you never tell it where to go. So it is with Bible study. We can study and chat about love all we want, but studying and even dialoguing about it doesn't constitute an effective decision. We must push the button to apply what we've learned to our everyday lives. Otherwise, our Bible study time is all for naught. Implementing change will look different from person to person, but the heart of the matter is the same: obedience. Applying Scripture to our lives involves an unwavering commitment to relentlessly follow where He leads.

RESPOND TO GOD'S WORD

1. Spend a few moments in heart preparation for today's time with God. Confess any tendencies to make application a checklist, instead of a pursuit of His presence. Ask God to show you what it looks like to apply His Word through a deeper faith in His goodness.

IDENTIFY: What's the main idea?

2. Write out 1 Corinthians 13:1–3 in your own words.

3. Read a commentary or study Bible to see how your observations from this week line up with the scholars. As you search the commentaries, ask God to make clear the meaning of any passages that are fuzzy to you. Record any additional observations below.

4. Give this section of 1 Corinthians a simple title.

If you still have any lingering questions about this week's verse, ask a trusted pastor, mentor, or friend what they think about the verse, or enter the online discussion at BibleStudyHub.com.

MODIFY: How do my beliefs and actions line up to this main idea?

Journal through the following questions:

• Is biblical love an everyday essential to your life, or an occasional accessory?

• Are there places of spiritual ineffectiveness or eternal insignificance in your life because of lovelessness?

GLORIFY: In light of this main idea, how can I realign my life to best reflect God's glory?

5. How could believing the truths about love discovered in 1 Corinthians 13:1–3 affect your everyday moments?

6. What adjustments can you make to glorify God in the way I show love this week?

Living out in the country has given me a new appreciation for the night sky. In the suburbs, you just can't enjoy the light of each star and the glow of the moon like you can out in the boonies. As a young child, I assumed the moon was a light of its own, shining down on us to light our night paths, but of course we all know that the moon is simply a satellite of the sun's rays. I often wonder if God gave us the moon for more than just a nightlight, as it's a perfect picture of how we can reflect God's character. The light of the moon does not come from itself; its illumination is merely a reflection of the glory of the sun, bringing light to the darkness. You and I are like that moon. We have no light of our own of which to boast. Any brightness that bounces off us, into the dark of this world, is from the supreme source of God's blazing glory.

You and I exist to bring glory to God. Application is not digging down deep within ourselves so we can try harder and do better, it is a realignment; a coming back to the One who is at work within us and allowing Him to do as He wills so that we can show Him glorious to those around us. Studying God's Word helps us see the adjustments we need to make in order to better depend on God and reflect His glory. Responding to all we learn in the Bible naturally leads to the light of God reflecting off us—His image bearers—on to a dark world desperate for the presence of God in their days.

> *I need You, God. I have no hope for change without Your grace. Help me to work and serve and love with an eternal perspective today.*

FOCUSING ON **1 CORINTHIANS 13:4–7**

The Evidence of Love

Foundation

FOCUSing ON 1 CORINTHIANS 13:4–7

Search me, O God, and know my heart! Try me and know my thoughts! And see if there be any grievous way in me, and lead me in the way everlasting!

—PSALM 139:23–24

A FEW YEARS ago, I received a diagnosis of an autoimmune disease. For the most part, it's under control but it means I can't eat gluten. I know, poor me. Living a gluten-free lifestyle becomes easier with the passing of each day, but there are certainly times where I miss my old favorites. At the top of the list are chocolate-covered pretzels, Red Lobster's biscuits, and Papa John's pizza. "Better ingredients. Better pizza. Papa John's." That's their company slogan and, in my opinion, it's true. Compared to other pizza brands, there is vast difference in the taste of the final product.

The quality ingredients in Papa John's pizza leads to a better quality tasting pizza. Likewise, the impressions we leave on those around us should point to the "better ingredients" inside of us. The Spirit of God dwells within every soul who places his or her faith in Jesus, and those who don't know Jesus should be able to get an accurate taste of God through every interaction with His people. Sometimes, however, Christians leave a horrible taste to those around them, instead of a satisfying one.

This week, we'll look at the characteristics seen when love is present in our lives. After illustrating in verses 1–3 that love is a critical component to our kingdom usefulness, significance, and rewards, Paul then gives evaluators for the Corinthians to consider—a thermometer of sorts. Paul wasn't trying to give a comprehensive definition of love in these verses. Remember, we've intercepted a conversation. Paul knew the specific struggles of the church and his words are corrective in nature. He wasn't giving them a "How to Love Better" checklist; he was giving them an evaluation test (which they failed), and thus a proverbial kick in the behind.

"You are the salt of the earth, but if salt has lost its taste, how shall its saltiness be restored? It is no longer good for anything except to be thrown out and trampled under people's feet" (Matthew 5:13).

1. Take some time to think about what you taste like to those around you who don't know God. Circle the words below that best describe your everyday life and interactions with others.

Patient	Exposes and exploits the mistakes of others
Kind	Assumes the worst about people
Content	Desires for others to fail
Modest	Writes people off once they've crossed the line
Humble	Discreet about other's mistakes
Considerate	Believes the best about people
Selfless	Hopes for the best for others
Impatient	Endures the offenses of others
Unkind	Selfish
Envious	Boastful
Arrogant	Rude

Though the verses we will study this week are most assuredly worthy attributes to aspire to, I think Paul's heart for these people (and God's heart for us) is not to turn this into a checklist. Instead, theses evaluators are to point us back to our need for Jesus, the perfect example of love. Instead of driving us to try harder; the truths we uncover are meant to compel us nearer to God. Because without His transforming work in our hearts, we will never become patient. Without His constant grace in our moments, we cannot be truly kind. Sacrificial love in not within reach without the enabling power of God's Spirit. The absence or presence of Jesus in our everyday moments will determine whether love is evidenced in our everyday movements. As we enter into this week's study, let's be on guard for the tendency to turn these verses into a checklist. Rather, let's use this as a gentle reminder of our desperate need for Christ, without whom we are incapable of biblical love.

2. Begin today's study with a prayer of dependence. Ask the Holy Spirit to open your eyes to the places where you are not living out biblical love. Confess them. Cling to the mercy and grace He gives today and every day.

ENJOY EVERY WORD

3. Begin your foundation work of 1 Corinthians 13:4–7 by writing, diagramming, or illustrating the passage below.

4. What stands out to you in 1 Corinthians 13:4–7? Do you have any questions about the passage?

It's necessary to take a regular inventory of my choices. How I spend my time, energy, and resources mirrors the state of my heart. I might say I want to be more patient with people, but my actions continually reflect another reality. Evaluation helps show me where what I truly want has been overturned by the impulsion and bad habits of my sinful soul. Without a fight, my flesh always wins. It's my depraved default to be impatient and selfish. Simply trying harder to be more lovingly patient doesn't work. As I see room for great improvement, I must choose to strive against my impatience, but it must be done out of a desire to draw near to God with faith that He will bring about change. I cannot make myself more loving, but Jesus can be perfectly loving through me.

> God, help me see where I am striving on my own to be more loving. I confess that I'd rather have a "how to love better" checklist of things to do. Draw my heart toward Yours. Enable me to love like Jesus, solely by faith in the work You have done in me and through the power of the Holy Spirit, not my own efforts.

⁙ BONUS STUDY ⁙

Work on memorizing 1 Corinthians 13:4–7. Write out the passage several times on notecards and post them around the house. Don't forget places where your hands are busy, but your mind is available. You could post a card up above your sink in the kitchen, or hang one up in the shower, housed in a plastic baggie. Time and effort spent toward stowing these verses in your heart will bring a great return.

Observation

FOCUSing ON 1 CORINTHIANS 13:4–7

Love is patient and kind.

—1 CORINTHIANS 13:4

LEST I THINK I've ever "arrived," it takes only a moment of stress to show me how far removed I am from biblical love. My everyday moments more often resemble lovelessness rather than the definition of biblical love. Over and over again I insist on my own way as I bark out commands in haste to my kids or speak short words to my husband and leave no room for doubt that I'm irritated. "If anyone thinks he is religious and does not bridle his tongue but deceives his heart, this person's religion is worthless" (James 1:26).

Impatience, at its core, is a love issue. The Greek word used in 1 Corinthians 13:4 for *patient* (makrothumeō) has the connotation of being slow to act against wrongdoing. Whereas the word *kind* (chrēsteue-tai) has a meaning of responding with a mild demeanor. These are reactive words. The challenge here is not to go out and be more patient and kind. Instead, love is displayed in our response to the offenses of others. When someone intentionally wrongs me or is just incredibly annoying, my response reveals love (or hate). I don't need to look far to find an occasion to love. I am given continual opportunities to love each and every day.

"For out of the abundance of the heart the mouth speaks" (Matthew 12:34).

God loved me so I can show love. "Not counting their trespasses against them, and entrusting to us the message of reconciliation" (2 Corinthians 5:19). God extended me mercy so I can extend mercy. God is patient with me so I can be patient with others. Once again, we have our example of love in our Savior. God's love for His people is patient. My sin—and yours—is a continual offense to a holy God. Yet, He responded to our offensive actions toward Him with love.

> *The Lord is not slow to fulfill his promise as some count slowness, but is patient* [makrothumeō] *toward you, not wishing that any should perish, but that all should reach repentance.*
>
> — 2 PETER 3:9

1. Open your time with Him through a prayer in the space below, expressing your eagerness to learn more about biblical love today.

LOOK AT THE DETAILS

2. Read 1 Corinthians 13:4–7, and pay close attention to what Paul states is true about love. Sort each truth about love in the chart provided.

LOVE IS . . .	LOVE IS NOT . . .	LOVE DOES . . .	LOVE DOES NOT . . .

3. Take a deeper look at each column in your chart. Do you see any similarities of the characteristics within each column? What about any distinctions or contrasts between them? Note any observations below. Consider creating a title for each group and write it below.

LOVE IS . . .	LOVE IS NOT . . .	LOVE DOES . . .	LOVE DOES NOT . . .

Love is evidenced in our responses to others. All too often, when we want to make changes in our lives, we go overboard looking for new things to help us in our journey. In our efforts to be intentional, we skip right over the simplest solution. Truth is, we already know what to do. We don't have to look far for ways to show love to others. Every moment we have to spend with the people God has planted us next to is an opportunity to love. From the next-door neighbor we rarely speak to to the girl at work who drives us crazy to the friends and family closest to us, as we choose to stay near to God and keep in step with His Spirit, He will faithfully enable us to love others and bear witness to the love we ourselves have experienced.

"For God so loved the world, that he gave his only Son, that whoever believes in him should not perish but have eternal life" (John 3:16).

God, I praise You for your extravagant love! I deserve judg-ment, yet You have lavished Your love on me. Jesus, thank You for taking the wrath of my sin so that I can experience the favor of my Creator. Spirit, enable me to respond with extravagant, patient, and kind love with every offense I face today.

⁙ BONUS STUDY ⁙

Spend some time observing truths about the love of God in the following passages.

JOHN 3:16	ROMANS 5:6–8	EPHESIANS 2:1–8	1 JOHN 4:9–10

CHEAT SHEET

2. Read 1 Corinthians 13:4–7, and pay close attention to what Paul states is true about love. Sort each truth about love in the chart provided.

LOVE IS . . .	LOVE IS NOT . . .	LOVE DOES . . .	LOVE DOES NOT . . .
patient kind	arrogant rude irritable resentful	rejoice with the truth bear all things believe all things hope all things endure all things	envy or boast insist on its own way rejoice at wrong-doings

3. Consider creating a title for each group and write it below.

LOVE IS . . .	LOVE IS NOT . . .	LOVE DOES . . .	LOVE DOES NOT . . .
the essence of love	the antithesis of love	the evidence of love	the evidence of lovelessness

Clarification

FOCUSing ON 1 CORINTHIANS 13:4–7

*Love . . . is not arrogant or rude . . . it is not irritable or
resentful.*

—1 Corinthians 13:4–5

I'M NOT EXACTLY sure when it started, but after years of small differences
and varied opinions, a beautiful friendship became toxic company in my
life. Over time, our problems affected my everyday thoughts and actions.
Where there was once love, rampant hate took its place. One day I could
no longer hold it all in as I exploded with frustration and fury (face down
in the beige Berber carpet of my bedroom) and threw a fit a three year
old would be proud of. At the time, I knew I must have had some part
to play in the degradation of the relationship, but I was blinded by my
pride and frustration to see my own sin. I messed things up good, and it
has taken me a very long time to realize where I went wrong. Hindsight
shows clearly the culprit of my relationship turned sour: resentment.

As we will see in today's study, the word *resentful* is a translation
of two Greek words. The first is *logizomai*, meaning "to count up," like
you do when you balance your checkbook. Nothing is let go without an
account. The second word, *kakos*, translates to "wrongdoing." Put these
two together, and you get resentment — counting up wrongdoings and
not letting anything go.

I've never considered myself a resentful person. I don't typically
look back at hurts and hold on to them. But in this situation, I did. I

had allowed the counting of wrongs to creep in. I carried a mental ledger for every blunder and breach my friend displayed—even if it wasn't specifically against me. Over time, this person could do no right in my eyes. I may have stated I loved this person, but the raw reality of my heart proved otherwise.

1. Spend some time today in contemplative prayer, asking God to reveal the places of hatred stored up in your heart.

If you find yourself in a strained relationship with a family member, co-worker, neighbor, or friend, I pray your heart would be open to the ugly reality of resentment, and the beautiful freedom that comes with choosing love and letting go of the ledger of wrongs you have toward that person. As we continue to study and store up the truths about biblical love—and act on them—you and I can avoid the toxicity of resentment.

UNCOVER THE ORIGINAL MEANING

There is much to dig through today, much more than a 15-minute session can hold. Remember, the daily study structure is simply a suggestion. You are in control of your own studies! If the Lord leads, feel free to take an additional day or two to dive into the original language in this passage. Additionally, if you are new to Bible study, you can always just look up each word in the dictionary and skip the Greek study.

Step 1: DECIDE which English word you would like to study.
Today, we will study the word resentful.

Step 2: DISCOVER the Greek word in an interlinear Bible.

Look up the word "resentful" (v. 5) in an interlinear Bible to find the original Greek word used and write it below.

resentful =

Step 3: DEFINE that Greek word using a Greek lexicon.

This one English word actually represents three Greek words. Did you find them? One of them, ό or "ho," is an article, like *the*. The other two words are deep with meaning. Let's learn more about both.

resentful = logizomai ho kakos

Lexicon study: logizomai

• Definition:

• Times used:

• Part of speech:

• Other ways it is translated:

• Any special notes:

Lexicon study: kakos

• Definition:

• Times used:

• Part of speech:

• Other ways it is translated:

• Any special notes:

2. What discoveries did you make through your clarification study? Which word did you learn the most about?

What I was just beginning to understand decades ago, and what I still strive to fully understand, is that I am continually at fault. In big ways and small, I daily add to my own ledger of sin debt. My account is in the red. A deep, negative red. "For the wages of sin is death" (Romans 6:23). Yet, because I am in Christ, God does not count my sins against me. There is no resentment in Christ. My wrongdoings are not counted up, instead, they are forgotten! "All this is from God, who through Christ reconciled us to himself . . . not counting their trespasses against them" (2 Corinthians 5:18–19). The word *counting* here is the same *logizomai* word used in 1 Corinthians 13. Through the sacrifice of Christ, and by the faith I placed in His work on the cross, God no longer counts my every sin against me. Halleluiah!

Though it does not take away the sting of the sin others commit against me, the reality of my own sin should move me toward love. Because a deep understanding of my own depravity keeps me from being surprised when I see that same depravity in others. Without the restraining hand of God's grace, I am worse than the very person who has wronged me most.

> *Jesus, I am so thankful for the incredible act of love You showed for me on the Cross. Without it I am hopeless, and unable to show love. I need You, Holy Spirit, to fill every crevasse of my heart. I submit my heart to You. Make it to love others like Christ loved me.*

⁎ BONUS STUDY ⁎

Look up additional words throughout each verse in this week's passage. If you are looking for recommendations, here are a few good places to start:

patient (v. 4)

rude (v. 5)

endures (v. 7)

Step 1: DECIDE which English word you would like to study.

Step 2: DISCOVER the Greek word in an interlinear Bible.

Step 3: DEFINE that Greek word using a Greek lexicon and note the following:

Lexicon discovery:

- Definition:
- Times used:
- Part of speech:
- Other ways it is translated:
- Any special notes:

Continue this process through as many words as you would like to study.

CHEAT SHEET

Step 3: DEFINE that Greek word using a Greek lexicon.

Lexicon study: logizomai

• Definition: keep mental record, charge to account, keep records of debits and credits

• Times used: 40

• Part of speech: verb

• Other ways it is translated: consider, reckon, count, think, impute

• Any special notes: Strong's #3049; "to reckon, count, compute, calculate, count over. to take into account, to make an account of. . . . to pass to one's account, to impute."

Lexicon study: kakos

• Definition: evil, bad

• Times used: 50

• Part of speech: adjective

• Other ways it is translated:

• Any special notes: Strong's #2556; "bad (immoral), wicked, wrong"

Utilization

FOCUSing ON 1 CORINTHIANS 13:4–7

Love bears all things, believes all things, hopes all things, endures all things.

—1 Corinthians 13:7

THE THREAT OF a house fire is haunting. Fire can spread quickly and in unpredictable ways, bringing a great potential for destruction. Though fire can be erratic, we do know there are three things needed for a fire to burn: heat, oxygen, and fuel. In light of this, safety experts suggest keeping a fire blanket handy at home, especially for small kitchen fires. A fire blanket is a nonflammable covering used to contain a small fire from getting out of control. It's designed to contain the fire by preventing oxygen access, thus smothering the fire into submission. The blanket provides a covering in order to suffocate the flames.

You and I have fires that pop up everyday, and they are (hopefully!) not in our kitchen. Every wrongdoing we experience is an ember, and we have an opportunity to smother it immediately or allow it to catch into a smoldering wildfire. Each insult, injury, or inconsideration encountered is a chance to cover the offender in love. However, when we focus on the little attacking flames on our doorstep we breathe life into it and allow it to burn bright, instead of immediately smothering the offense with love.

As we will see today in God's words to us, love covers. It quickly blows out the flame of irritability, resentment, and pride. Again and again and again. It suffers long toward every ember that tempts to take

over. Once again, love is shown in the response we make
toward wrongdoing. We don't need to go out looking for fires to put out,
we each have enough to go around. Fires pop up every day, and in those
moments when we begin to feel the heat, we have a choice to feed the fire
or smother it into submission.

1. Ask God to give you a greater awareness of the little fires in your life that
you've allowed to become a damaging wildfire.

DISCOVER THE CONNECTIONS

2. Read 1 Corinthians 13:4–7 to start your study today, then look up each
reference below and record what you learn from any passages that reveal a
bigger picture of the threads this verse is attached to.

13:4—"love is patient"

Proverbs 10:12

Proverbs 17:9

1 Peter 4:8

Jesus smothered sin into submission. His love covered over you and me in a way we cannot fully comprehend on this side of eternity. And as we attempt to grasp the reality of Christ's covering, let's move toward extending that gospel covering to those around us as extravagantly as Christ did for us.

"I will greatly rejoice in the LORD; my soul shall exult in my God, for he has clothed me with the garments of salvation; he has covered me with the robe of righteousness" (Isaiah 61:10).

> *Jesus, I praise You for Your covering of grace and forgiveness. Never let me forget what You have saved me from. Help me to see the fires that need covering and enable me to douse them with love today.*

∴ BONUS STUDY ∴

Look up the cross-references for additional phrases in each verse in this week's passage. Continue on until you need to move on with your day. If your Bible does not have cross-references in it, check out the online cross-references recommendations at KatieOrr.me/Resources. You could easily spend two or three days, 15 minutes or more at a time, working through each verse. Remember, these days are simply suggestions. Follow God's leading. If He tells you to slow down and dig deep, go for it!

CHEAT SHEET

2. Read 1 Corinthians 13:4–7 to start your study today, then look up each reference below and record what you learn from any passages that reveal a bigger picture of the threads this verse is attached to.

13:4—"love is patient"

Proverbs 10:12

Love covers all offenses.

Proverbs 17:9

Whoever covers an offense seeks love,

1 Peter 4:8

Love covers a multitude of sins.

Summation

FOCUSing ON 1 CORINTHIANS 13:4–7

For if anyone is a hearer of the word and not a doer, he is like
a man who looks intently at his natural face in a mirror. For
he looks at himself and goes away and at once forgets what
he was like.

—JAMES 1:23–24

BEFORE I LEAVE the house, I often give myself one last look in the mirror. I've had way too many experiences of returning home from an event to notice lipstick on my teeth, my shirt on inside out, or realize I forgot to put eyeliner on. (No wonder everyone kept asking me if I was tired!) The mirror gives me instant feedback to know that I can walk into a group setting without fear of unnecessary embarrassment. My kids, however, don't usually look in the mirror before they leave the house. Oftentimes they walk out with mismatched outfits and disheveled hair if I don't catch them in time. Part of growing up is developing a healthy awareness of self, not only for our external appearance, but for our emotional and spiritual maturity as well.

The summer after my freshman year of college, I took the Myers-Briggs personality assessment test during a missions trip with over 80 other college students. Out of all the young adults there, only one other had the same personality combination as me: the one person in the group I least enjoyed being around. She was obnoxious, over-confident, and obviously needed a steady stream of attention from others. Turns out, so was I. After making the connection that her personality mirrored my own, I was given the gift of a greater self-awareness of my own social weaknesses. It was a painful realization, and I've since had many other eye-opening experiences that have led toward a better understanding of how I treat people. Though it is not always fun to look in the mirror to see the ugliness inside, I am thankful for every step toward a deeper discernment of how well (or poorly) I reflect the image of Christ to those around me.

Through the verses we've studied this week, Paul provided a mirror for the immature church at Corinth. They were walking around dishonoring the name of Christ by their lack of self-awareness of how they looked to the lost world around them. It takes only a quick glance at a Facebook feed to see that the church today could use a long refining look at their reflection. As representatives of our God, the love of Christ should be unmistakable in our lives, and 1 Corinthians 13:4–7 is a good place to start for each of us to see how well our daily impression compares to the likeness of biblical love.

RESPOND TO GOD'S WORD

1. Spend a few moments of quiet prayer, in preparation for today's summation time with God. Declare to Him your desire to respond in obedient worship to all you've learned this week.

IDENTIFY: What's the main idea?

2. Write out 1 Corinthians 13:4–7 in your own words.

3. Read a commentary or study Bible to see how your observations on this passage line up with the scholars. As you search the commentaries, ask God to make clear the meaning of any passages that are fuzzy to you. Record any additional observations.

4. Give this section a title.

If you still have any lingering questions about this week's verse, ask a trusted pastor, mentor, or friend what they think about the verse, or enter the online discussion at BibleStudyHub.com.

MODIFY: How do my beliefs line up to this main idea?

Journal through the following questions:

5. How does your view of how to truly love others line up with what you've learned this week?

6. What is your typical, initial response to those who wrong you?

7. Do you tend to count up the wrongdoings of others or cover them with love?

GLORIFY: In light of this main idea, how can I realign my life to best reflect God's glory?

8. How could believing the truths discovered in 1 Corinthians 13:4–7 affect your everyday moments?

9. What adjustments can you make to glorify God in your attitudes and actions this week?

Love is characterized by persevering the offenses of others and showing kindness to the one who offends. Love does not boil with envy or put itself on display. Love does not demand its own way. It is not irritable. It does not resent. It does not enjoy sin, but rejoices in what is right. Love is a protective covering, as it weathers through all storms that come. Love has great confidence in people, with a deep commitment toward them through whatever they may go through. Love has a confident expectation for good things to come and believes the best of people. Love remains, even when the unthinkable happens.

This list of love can be overwhelming, and I can't help but feeling discouraged, as I am so far removed from the likeness of Christlike love. But just as it would be silly for me to look in the mirror to find something hanging from my nose and leave it there, I must be careful not to leave this week's study and not take care of what is lacking in my everyday love. I must remember that through the enabling power of the Spirit, I can love better. Where there is selfishness, envy, pride, and impatience, God can produce a kind, patient, enduring love. When I am weary of my loveless living, I can choose to depend on His gracious and powerful work within me, and pray toward His will for me to be a love-filled image of Christ. As I do this, He can (and will) create a newness in my heart toward love. Because it's His will that we love others well.

And this is the confidence that we have toward him, that if we ask anything according to his will he hears us. And if we know that he hears us in whatever we ask, we know that we have the requests that we have asked of him.

—1 JOHN 5:14–15

God, I long for those around me to experience Your loving hand through my actions. By Your grace, help me to respond with love today.

FOCUSING ON **1 CORINTHIANS 13:8–13**

Love Is Eternal

Foundation

FOCUSing ON 1 CORINTHIANS 13:8–13

WHEN WE PURCHASED our new-to-us used Kia Sedona back in 2007, it was still under warranty. It was our first big car purchase as a couple and we spent many hours researching and preparing for the acquisition. With our oldest child almost two and our secondborn on the way, this light blue minivan quickly became an integral part of our family life. The Kia has been good to us, but with over 154,000 miles on it and seven years of our family's use (and abuse), our everyday vehicle is tired. The manual sliding doors don't glide the way they used to, the gray carpet and cup-holders are stained and sticky, and the air conditioning leaks freon.

We've recently had to evaluate if it is worth investing any more money in it through repairs. We are not eager to get into a car payment, yet we don't want to throw our money into a van that will most likely be in the scrapyard before long. As much as we wish it would, our beloved minivan will not last forever. Yet in our search for a new vehicle, it has become all too easy to get wrapped up into all the fancy features that make everyday life easier. While these luxuries are not sinful, if we are not careful, they can soften our resolve to live with an eternal perspective. This earth is not our home. Our steady paycheck, physical health, and everyday moments are gifts from our Creator, each meant to be stewarded for His glory, not used for our comfort.

Do not lay up for yourselves treasures on earth, where moth and rust destroy and where thieves break in and steal, but lay up for yourselves treasures in heaven, where neither moth nor rust destroys and where thieves do not break in and steal.

—MATTHEW 6:19–20

The way we live our lives matters for eternity. One day, we will stand before our beautiful Savior and offer up to Him all that was done in love. Because love is eternal. It will last forever, and though we are so easily distracted by everything the world throws our way to keep us from loving others for His glory, love is what we will do for eternity. Why not get started today?

1. Pray and ask God to give you His strength to endure in your love efforts. Ask Him for the grace to see His love in these verses, and then choose well today as you apply them.

ENJOY EVERY WORD

2. Work through your first layer of studying 1 Corinthians 13:8–13 by writing the passage below in the way you enjoy best:

3. What stands out to you in 1 Corinthians 13:8–13? Do you have any questions about the passage?

After months of deliberation, we finally decided on a black, shiny Toyota Camry, and after only a month into owning it, we were T-boned at a highway intersection. Our new car was destroyed in an instant. The crash itself happened at what seemed like light-speed, but the whirling out of control across the highway felt like an eternity. It was as if we were floating around in the air like Forrest Gump's feather until we landed safely in the middle of the median wildflowers.

As soon as I realized that red SUV was heading toward the middle of the intersection—and directly at us—all I could do was slam on my breaks and plead for God's mercy. *Keep my babies safe.* During the crash, and the terrifying moments afterward, my primary concern was not our new Camry, it was my children. Are they breathing? Do they have all their limbs intact? Did they sustain any injuries? As soon as the car stopped spinning I immediately looked back at those three precious souls and could not be happier to see each of them squirming in the backseat. We climbed out of the car, I confirmed that they were all completely intact with only tiny bruises and abrasions, then comforted them. Together we huddled amidst the shards of glass and wild purple perennials and praised God for His grace.

The Camry, though it was shiny and new, is temporary and insignificant in light of eternity. The souls of my children will live forever, and the way I love them is incredibly significant. The same is true for every person on this planet. Cars and houses and smartphones will all pass away. Family and neighbors and co-workers will not, and they were each created to know and experience the love of God, and you and I are placed amidst them to bear witness to God's purpose for their lives. Today, let's give our time, talents, and treasures toward loving infinite souls instead of finite stuff.

Lord, I need You. I am easily discouraged by my lack of love for others and distracted by the lures of this world. Give me the eternal perspective needed to press on when loving others is difficult. Help me fix my eyes on You, draw near to Your presence, hold on to the hope of good things to come, and love extravagantly.

⁓ BONUS STUDY ⁓

Continue your memory work of this passage, this week add 1 Corinthians 13:8–13.

Observation

FOCUSing ON 1 CORINTHIANS 13:8–13

Then I shall know fully, even as I have been fully known.

—1 CORINTHIANS 13:12

IF YOU ENJOY puzzles and logic problems, you'll love Monument Valley. Available for most mobile devices, this game takes you on a quest with a sweet wanderer, Ida. To play, you must tell Ida where to go next in order to help her on her trek, but you soon learn that the rules are different in Ida's world. At first glance, there seems to be no way to get Ida from point A to point B. Until you learn that she can walk on the walls— upside down, even—and that you can manipulate the paths in unex- pected ways, opening up a passage you didn't see before. Monument Valley is an elaborate optical illusion and continually forces you to think outside the box.

My kids downloaded the game on my phone and I got sucked in. It took me a while to figure it out, as my understanding of the way things worked in Ida's world was limited. It almost led me to give up on the game altogether until my eyes were opened to a different dimension of the game that was needed for my problem solving. This new understand- ing allowed me to solve the puzzles ahead.

Similarly, our comprehension of God and His ways is limited on this side of eternity. Yet God, in all wisdom, has allowed this limitation. Paul states this fact in 1 Corinthians 13 for our benefit. It is helpful to know that what we see is not all of what we get. There is so much more to the story than we can ever imagine.

1. Open your time with Him through a prayer, expressing your eagerness to see Him more clearly today.

LOOK AT THE DETAILS

2. Read 1 Corinthians 13:8–13, and look for the contrast between the temporary and the eternal. As you observe truths about that which is temporary, write it out in the "temporary" column. Do the same with any statements of that which is eternal.

TEMPORARY	ETERNAL

3. Which of these contrasting truths stand out to you?

I find it very interesting that Paul included the last phrase in verse 12 "even as I have been fully known." He could have made the point that our knowledge and understanding is hindered on this side of heaven. But Paul includes this descriptive phrase of his experience—the intimacy of being fully known. God knows the number of hairs on our head (even the gray ones I attempt to cover). He sees every tear that falls from our eyes; even before the womb He knew us. David, the psalmist, is right to declare "such knowledge is too wonderful for me" (Psalm 139:6). Just as God intimately knows and loves us, we will fully know the presence of God and with it will come the full knowledge and understanding of His purposes and plan set forth from the beginning of time. All will be enlightened. Every question answered. Every hope fulfilled.

> *O Lᴏʀᴅ, you have searched me and known me! You know when I sit down and when I rise up; you discern my thoughts from afar. You search out my path and my lying down and are acquainted with all my ways. Even before a word is on my tongue, behold, O Lᴏʀᴅ, you know it altogether. You hem me in, behind and before, and lay your hand upon me. Such knowledge is too wonderful for me; it is high; I cannot attain it.*
>
> —Psᴀʟᴍ 139:1–6

I must be on guard for the limiting presuppositions I bring when I attempt to comprehend God's ways and commands. When I'm tempted to want an explanation for every question that pops in my head, I must remember I am finite, but God is infinite. My knowledge and capacity to love is limited but His is limitless. I am weak but He is strong.

> *God, grant me this eternal perspective. Especially when I wonder or worry about the past or future, give me great faith to trust in Your great and faithful character. I'm thankful that I don't have to have all the answers. I just have to have You.*

⁖ BONUS STUDY ⁖

Look up these additional verses on being known by God, and record what you learn.

1 CORINTHIANS 8:1–3	2 TIMOTHY 2:19	ISAIAH 43:1	JEREMIAH 1:5

CHEAT SHEET

2. Read 1 Corinthians 13:8–13, and look for the contrast between the temporary and the eternal. As you observe truths about that which is temporary, write it out in the "temporary" column. Do the same with any statements of that which is eternal.

TEMPORARY	ETERNAL
Prophecies will pass away	Love never ends
Tongues will cease	The perfect is coming
Knowledge will pass away	When I became a man • I gave up childish ways • Then face to face
We know in part	
We prophesy in part	Then I shall know fully even as I have been fully known
The partial will pass away	
When I was a child: • I spoke like a child • I thought like a child • I reasoned like a child	Faith, hope, and love abide
Now we see in a mirror dimly	
Now I know in part	

Clarification

FOCUSing ON 1 CORINTHIANS 13:8–13

When I was a child, I spoke like a child, I thought like a child, I reasoned like a child. When I became a man, I gave up child-ish ways.

—1 CORINTHIANS 13:11

I LOVE MEXICAN food. Growing up in southern California, there were no shortage of amazing and affordable Mexican restaurants. These days, the Orr family has a standing Sunday lunch date with two orders of sizzling fajitas to share.

One of my favorite things about eating Mexican food is the guacamole. Avocados require very little preparation or additional ingredients to make great guacamole, assuming you have the right avocado. First off, they must be Haas avocados (none of those Florida avocados!), and they must be perfectly ripe. My seven-year-old daughter also loves guacamole and can make it on her own, but still needs me to tell her when the avocado is dip-ready; if she cuts into it too soon, it's a waste. Though she is often eager to make guacamole, she's learned that she must wait until the avocado is perfectly ripe if she wants a good tasting bowl of guacamole.

We too must learn to wait. We are living in the not-ripe-yet days, waiting for God's glory to be fully revealed in His perfect timing—the perfect maturity of God's plan. You and I are immature. Whether we've walked with God for days or decades, we are each being perfected in the image of Christ. This is a process that will continue until the day we see

Jesus face to face. Compared to all God will complete in us in heaven, we're crawling along in infancy.

In the meantime, God has given us spiritual gifts as crutches to help us toddle toward eternity. And because we all have much maturing to do, we need the uniqueness of each other's gifts as we strive toward knowing God better and reflecting His glory to a world who is in desperate need for a Savior. However, our spiritual gifts will end. They are a temporary provision, and if I attempt to make them my identity or a reason for pride, I miss the purpose of why they were instated—to serve other believers in Christ as we journey toward eternity together. When my salvation is complete, and I stand before Jesus, I will be perfectly, completely mature. The need for my spiritual gifts will have ended.

1. Take a moment to think through your own spiritual gifts. What has God made you really good at? Write them down below.

2. Now, take a close look at your heart's posture toward these talents. Do you tend to find your significance and worth attached to these abilities? How are you using these gifts to love others around you?

UNCOVER THE ORIGINAL MEANING

How is this Greek study thing going for you? I hope today you find it a bit easier and are more at home than when we first started studying together.

Step 1: DECIDE which English word you would like to study. Today, we will study the word perfect.

Step 2: DISCOVER the Greek word in an interlinear Bible. Look up the word "perfect" (v. 10) in an interlinear Bible to find the original Greek word used and write it below.

perfect =

Step 3: DEFINE that Greek word using a Greek lexicon.

Lexicon study:

• Definition:

• Times used:

• Part of speech:

• Other ways it is translated:

• Any special notes:

3. What discoveries did you make through your clarification study?

Children tend to think they know and understand a whole lot more than they do. This is cute as a five year old, not so much as an adult. In light of eternity, you and I are a tiny blip—a vapor. When we think of ourselves as bigger, brighter, or more mature than we really are, we take away from the glory due His name. We are infantile compared to the grandeur of God, and any gift granted by Him is to be used to point others to Christ alone.

> *He is my steadfast love and my fortress, my stronghold and my deliverer, my shield and he in whom I take refuge . . . O LORD, what is man that you regard him, or the son of man that you think of him? Man is like a breath; his days are like a passing shadow.*
>
> —PSALM 144:2–4

God, grant me a right perspective on my spiritual gifts. Help me to use them while I am able, but not to let them define or limit me. I pray You would use me to glorify You to those around me.

⸱!⸱ BONUS STUDY ⸱!⸱

Look up additional words throughout each verse in this week's passage. A few to choose from are below.

- will pass away (v. 10)
- dimly (v. 12)
- know fully (v. 12)

Step 1: DECIDE which English word you would like to study.

Step 2: DISCOVER the Greek word in an interlinear Bible.

Step 3: DEFINE that Greek word using a Greek lexicon.

Look up that Greek word in a Greek lexicon (which is like a dictionary) and note the following:

Lexicon discovery:

• Definition:

• Times used:

• Part of speech:

• Other ways it is translated:

• Any special notes:

Continue this process through as many words as you would like to study.

CHEAT SHEET

Step 2: DISCOVER the Greek word in an interlinear Bible. Look up the word "perfect" (v. 10) in an interlinear Bible to find the original Greek word used and write it below.

perfect = teleios

Step 3: DEFINE that Greek word using a Greek lexicon.

Lexicon study: teleios

• Definition: perfect; complete

• Times used: 19

• Part of speech: adjective

• Other ways it is translated: mature, full, genuine, complete

• Any special notes: Strong's #5046; "brought to its end, finished."

Utilization

FOCUSing ON 1 CORINTHIANS 13:8–13

For now we see in a mirror dimly, but then face to face. Now I know in part; then I shall know fully, even as I have been fully known.

—1 CORINTHIANS 13:12

TWO OF MY children are in a mommy phase. What I mean by that is they want to be with me all the time. They desire to be held by me, sit by me at every meal, and for me to pour their cereal (not Daddy)! And despite my best attempts at keeping my mattress kid free, they often sneak into my bed at night, just to stay close.

Since I've had at least one child in this mommy phase for almost a decade now, I've had to be creative to get certain things done. In order to find quiet moments to spend with God, carve out time to write, or even go to the bathroom on my own takes a bit of effort. Recently, I've made attempts to get out of the house to exercise during the early morning hours, yet I keep forgetting to set out what I need the night before. So I find myself fumbling around in the dark, trying to put together all my exercise gear without waking up the kids. Sometimes that means I arrive at the gym donning my shirt inside out, without a water bottle, and missing my sport headphones. Since I can barely see a foot in front of me, I struggle to find what I need for my trip to the gym.

As we'll see in our passage today, we're currently living in the dark when compared to eternity. It's as if we're trying to view a road map by the light of the moon alone or trying to match an outfit in the dark. Now we see dimly but one sweet day, we will see face to face. "The light of a candle is perfectly obscured by the sun shining in its strength" (Matthew Henry).

1. Open up today's time with God through a prayer of enlightenment. Ask God to guide you as you flip through the pages of His Word today.

DISCOVER THE CONNECTIONS

2. Read 1 Corinthians 13:8–13 to start your study today. Look up each reference below and take notes on what you learn.

v. 12—"now we see in a mirror dimly"

2 Corinthians 3:18

2 Corinthians 4:18

2 Corinthians 5:7

v. 12—"face to face"

1 John 3:2

There is much about eternity I can't get my mind around. Yet the Bible is clear, this world is a shadow and our lives are but a mist. The pleasures we experience on earth pale in comparison to all we'll experience in the unfettered presence of God. Sin will be abolished. Pain and sorrow gone. All things bright and shiny that catch our attention these days cannot hold a candle to the surpassing glory of God and His love for us.

God, You are glorious! I long to see more of You. Show me Your glory! More and more each day, reveal Yourself to me. And may I be forever changed by Your presence.

⁙ BONUS STUDY ⁙

Follow the cross-references for additional phrases in each verse of this week's passage.

CHEAT SHEET

2. Read 1 Corinthians 13:8–13 to start your study today. Look up each reference below and take notes on what you learn.

v. 12—"now we see in a mirror dimly"

2 Corinthians 4:18
What we see in our everyday is transient. There are things we cannot see that are eternal.

2 Corinthians 5:7
There is much about God that is yet to be seen. We walk in faith of all that is to come.

v. 12 —"face to face"

1 John 3:2
Though we are part of God's family now, when Jesus returns, we will be transformed to be just like Him, and we will see Jesus fully.

Summation

FOCUSing ON 1 CORINTHIANS 13:8–13

So now faith, hope, and love abide, these three; but the great-
est of these is love.

—1 CORINTHIANS 13:13

PAUL'S DONE THE summarizing for us. If we haven't had it hammered into our hearts by now, he lays it all out in 1 Corinthians 13:13. Love is supreme. Through the sacrifice of Christ, we can draw near to God by faith in His goodness. As we sojourn through our days toward eternity with our Savior, we must hold fast to our hope in the gospel and all the promises we have in Him. And it all culminates in love.

Love is greatest because it is eternal. When we meet Jesus face-to-face, faith will be complete because there will be no more need to draw near. Our faith will be made sight. We will be as near to God as we can ever be. Additionally, no longer will we need to hold on to hope, because all we've hoped for will be realized in heaven. All that will remain is love. Love for each other, but more importantly, an all-encompassing love for God. A love that will bring us to our knees in gratitude, worship, and awe.

RESPOND TO GOD'S WORD

1. Praise God today for His great love for us, by which we can experience the completion of our faith and the fulfillment of our hope in Christ.

IDENTIFY: What's the main idea?

2. Write out the main idea of 1 Corinthians 13:8–13.

3. Read a commentary or study Bible to see how your observations line up. As you search the commentaries, ask God to make clear the meaning of any passages that are fuzzy to you. Record any additional observations.

4. Give this section of 1 Corinthians 13 a title.

If you still have any lingering questions about this week's verse, ask a trusted pastor, mentor, or friend what they think about the verse, or enter the online discussion at BibleStudyHub.com.

MODIFY: How do my beliefs line up to this main idea?

Journal through the following questions:

5. How does your view of the eternality of love line up with what you've learned this week?

6. How does knowing your understanding is limited help you to love others better?

7. How does the reality of the temporary nature of spiritual gifts and all you can achieve on this earth help you to better show love to those around you?

8. Are you honest about the reality that the view from here is limited?

GLORIFY: In light of this main idea, how can I realign my life to best reflect God's glory?

9. How could believing the truths discovered in 1 Corinthians 13:8–13 affect your everyday moments?

10. What adjustments can you make to glorify God in your attitudes and actions this week?

Love. Love is God's gift to us, by which we experience the very one who carefully created us. Love is Christ's demonstration for us, which we can look to as a model for our lives as we turn our hearts toward His example. Love is the Spirit's fruit in us, through which we can walk in confidence that God is indeed at work in us. Love is the very mark of God on us, by which we bear witness to others of His goodness and grace, that they too might become part of the family of God.

Love is the expected evidence of a thriving, intimate walk with Jesus. Love is not a box on our checklist we try to accomplish, but a response we make to those around, especially those who offend us and are difficult to love. And as we supernaturally love others, the very character of God is experienced through our interactions. And though our reality is obscured, limited, and immature, we know that the love of God in us and through us never ends and every ounce of effort we put forth to bearing witness of Christ by loving others will be used by God to bring many souls to experience His glory.

> *God, help me to keep an eternal perspective. Where I am full of pride, humble me. Where my view is limited, help me to see. Where I cannot understand, show me Your glory. Thank You for loving me. Help me to love with an eternal, supernatural love that comes only from Your Spirit at work in me.*

Appendix

A Note from Katie

Thank you for taking this journey of love with me. I pray you hold a better understanding of biblical, everyday love as a result of going through this study. It is an honor to walk alongside of you as we strive together to be genuine, fruitful image bearers of God to the world around us.

Glossary of Bible Study Terms

Interlinear Bible: a translation where each English word is linked to its original Greek word. There are many free interlinear Bibles online, as well as great apps you can download to your phone or tablet. Check out KatieOrr.me/Resources for current links.

Concordance: a helpful list of words found in the original languages of the Bible (mainly Hebrew and Greek) and the verses where you can find them.

Cross-reference: a notation in a Bible verse that indicates there are other passages that contain similar material.

Footnote: a numerical notation that refers readers to the bottom of a page for additional information.

Commentary: a reference book written by experts that explains the Bible. A good commentary will give you historical background and language information that may not be obvious from the passage.

Greek: the language in which most of the New Testament was written.

Hebrew: the language in which most of the Old Testament was written

Structure and Books of the Bible

Books of the Law (also
known as the Pentateuch)

Genesis

Exodus

Leviticus

Numbers

Deuteronomy

Books of History

Joshua

Judges

Ruth

1 Samuel

2 Samuel

1 Kings

2 Kings

1 Chronicles

2 Chronicles

Ezra

Nehemiah

Esther

Wisdom Literature

Job

Psalms

Proverbs

Ecclesiastes

Song of Songs

Major Prophets

Isaiah

Jeremiah

Lamentations

Ezekiel

Daniel

Minor Prophets

Hosea

Joel

Amos

Obadiah

Jonah

Micah

Nahum

Habakkuk

Zephaniah

Haggai

Zechariah

Malachi

New Testament (First four together are known as "The Gospels")

Matthew

Mark

Luke

John

Acts

Epistles (or Letters) by Paul

Romans

1 Corinthians

2 Corinthians

Galatians

Ephesians

Philippians

Colossians

1 Thessalonians

2 Thessalonians

1 Timothy

2 Timothy

Titus

Philemon

General Epistles (Letters not by Paul)

Hebrews

James

1 Peter

2 Peter

1 John

2 John

3 John

Jude

Apocalyptic Writing

Revelation

Major Themes of the Bible

Though many view Scripture as a patchwork of historical accounts, morality tales, and wisdom for daily living, the Bible is really only one story—the mind-blowing story of God's plan to rescue fallen humanity. This storyline flows through every single book, chapter, verse, and word of Scripture. It's crucial that we know the movements, or themes, of the grand storyline so we don't miss the point of the passage we are studying.

For example, I grew up hearing about the story of David's adulterous affair with the beautiful, but married, Bathsheba. I heard how he covered his misdeeds with a murderous plot to snuff out her husband. This story was usually punctuated with a moral that went something like this, "Don't take what isn't yours!" While it is indeed good practice to refrain from taking what isn't ours, there is a much bigger connection to the grand story that we will miss if we stop at a moral lesson. So what then is this grand story, and how can we recognize it?

The story falls into four main themes, or movements: creation, fall, redemption, and completion*.

CREATION

The Bible begins by describing the creative work of God. His masterwork and crowning achievement was the creation of people. God put the first couple, Adam and Eve, in absolute paradise and gave them everything they needed to thrive. The best part of this place, the Garden of Eden, was that God walked among His people. They knew Him and were known by Him. The Bible even says they walked around naked because they had no concept of shame or guilt. (See Genesis 2:25.) Life was perfect, just like God had designed.

FALL

In the Garden, God provided everything for Adam and Eve. But He also gave them instructions for how to live and established boundaries for their protection. Eventually, the first family decided to cross the boundary, and break the one rule God commanded them to keep. This decision was the most fateful error in history. At that precise moment, paradise was lost. The connection people experienced with God vanished. Adam and Eve's act was not simply a mistake but outright rebellion against the sovereign creator of the universe. It was, in no uncertain terms, a declaration of war against God. Every aspect of creation was fractured in that moment. Because of their choice, Adam and Eve introduced death and disease to the world, but more importantly, put a chasm between mankind and God that neither Adam nor Eve nor any person could ever hope to cross. Ever since the fall, all people are born with a tendency to sin. Like moths to a light, we are drawn to sin, and like Adam and Eve, our sin pushes us further away from any hope of experiencing God. You see God cannot be good if he doesn't punish sin, but if we all receive the punishment our sin deserves we would all be cast away from Him forever.

REDEMPTION

Fortunately, God was not caught off guard when Adam and Eve rebelled. God knew they would and had a plan in place to fix what they had broken. This plan meant sending Jesus to earth. Even though Jesus was the rightful King of all creation, He came to earth in perfect humility. He walked the earth for more than 30 years experiencing everything you and I do. Jesus grew tired at the end of a long day. He got hungry when

He didn't eat. He felt the pain of losing loved ones, and the disappointment of betrayal from friends. He went through all of life like we do with one massive exception—He never sinned. Jesus never disobeyed God, not even once. Because He was without sin, He was the only one in history who could bridge the gap between God and us. However, redemption came at a steep price. Jesus was nailed to a wooden cross and left to die a criminal's death. While He hung on the Cross, God put the full weight of our sin upon Jesus. When the King of the universe died, He paid the penalty for our sin. God poured out His righteous anger toward our sin on the sinless One. After Jesus died, He was buried and many believed all hope was lost. However, Jesus did not stay dead—having defeated sin on the Cross, He was raised from death and is alive today!

COMPLETION

The final theme in the grand storyline of the Bible is completion, the end of the story. Now that Jesus has paid the penalty for our sin, we have hope of reconciliation with God. This is such tremendous news because reconciliation means we are forgiven of sin and given eternal life. Reconciliation means that God dwells with us again. Finally, we know Him and are known by Him. Completion for us means entering into reconciliation with God through the only means He provided. We can only experience reconciliation under God's rescue plan if we trust Jesus to pay for our sin, and demonstrate this by repenting, or turning away, from our sin. But God's rescue plan does not end with us. One day, Jesus will come back and ultimately fix every part of fallen creation. King Jesus will come back to rule over God's people, and again establish a paradise that is free from the effects of sin.

Let's return to the David and Bathsheba story for a moment and try to find our place. David was the greatest, most godly king in the history of the Old Testament, but even he was affected by the fall and had a sinful nature. This story points out that what we really need is not a more disciplined eye, but a total transformation. We need to be delivered from the effects of the fall. It also illustrates how we don't simply need a king who loves God, but we need a King who is God. Do you see how this story connects to the arc of the grand storyline? Just look at how much glorious truth we miss out on if we stop short at "don't take what isn't yours."

*For a more detailed discussion on these themes, refer to Part 1 and 2 of *The Explicit Gospel* by Matt Chandler (pages 21–175) or Chapter 2 of Mark Dever's *The Gospel and Personal Evangelism* (pages 31–44).

How to Do a Greek Word Study

Learning more about the language used in the original version of Scripture can be a helpful tool toward a better understanding of the author's original meaning and intention in writing.

STEP 1: DECIDE which English word you would like to study.

Do a quick read of your passage and note any potential keywords and/or repeated words. There is no right or wrong way to do this! Simply select a few words you would like to learn more about.

STEP 2: DISCOVER the Greek word in an interlinear Bible.

Using an interlinear Bible (see glossary), find the original Greek word for each instance of the word in the passage you are studying. There may be more than one Greek word present.

STEP 3: DEFINE the Greek word using a Greek lexicon.

Look up your Greek word (or words if you found more than one) in a Greek lexicon (see glossary).

Continue through these three steps for each word you would like to study.

Truths About Love Master Sheet

Use this space to record all truths discovered about love.

TRUTHS ABOUT LOVE

The Good News

GOD LOVES YOU

You are known and deeply loved by a great, glorious, and personal God. This God hand-formed you for a purpose (Ephesians 2:10), He has called you by name (Isaiah 43:1) and you are of great worth to Him (Luke 12:6–7).

WE HAVE A SIN PROBLEM

We are all sinners and are all therefore separated from God (Romans 3:23; 6:23). Even the "smallest" of sins is a great offense to God. He is a righteous judge who will not be in the presence of sin, and cannot allow sin to go unpunished. Our natural tendency toward sin has left us in desperate need of rescue because God must deal with our sin.

JESUS IS THE ONLY SOLUTION

Since God's standard is perfection, and we have all fallen short of the mark, Jesus is the *only* answer to our sin problem (John 14:6). Jesus lived a life of perfect obedience to God. So when Jesus died on the Cross, He alone was able to pay the penalty of our sin. After His death, Jesus rose from the dead, defeating death, and providing the one way we could be reconciled to God (2 Corinthians 5:17–21). Jesus Christ is the only one who can save us from our sins.

WE MUST CHOOSE TO BELIEVE

Trusting Christ is our only part in the gospel. Specifically, the Bible requires us to have faith in what Christ has done on our behalf (Ephesians 2:8–9). This type of faith is not just belief in God. Many people grow up believing that God exists but never enter into the Christian faith. Faith that saves comes from a desperate heart. A heart that longs for Jesus—the only solution for their sin problem—to be first and foremost in their life. We demonstrate that we have this type of saving faith by turning away, or repenting, from our sin.

FOCUSed15 Study Method

Apply this method to 2–10 verses a day, over a week's time, for a deep encounter with God through His Word, in as little as 15 minutes a day.

Foundation: Enjoy Every Word

Read and rewrite the passage—Summarize, draw pictures, sentence-diagram, or simply copy the passage. Do whatever helps you slow down and enjoy each word.

Observation: Look at the Details

Take notes on what you see—Write down what is true in this passage. Look for truths about the character of God, promises to cling to, or commands given.

Clarification: Uncover the Original Meaning

- Decide which English word to study.
- Discover the Hebrew word in an interlinear Bible.
- Define that Hebrew word using a Hebrew lexicon.

Utilization: Discover the Connections in Scripture

Cross-reference—Look up the references in each verse to view the threads and themes throughout the Bible.

Summation: Respond to God's Word

- Identify the main idea of each passage.
- Modify my beliefs to the truths found in this passage.
- Glorify God by aligning my life to reflect the truths I've discovered.

Use the QR reader on your
smartphone to visit us online at
NewHopePublishers.com

If you've been blessed by this book, we would like to hear your story.
The publisher and author welcome your comments and
suggestions at: newhopereader@wmu.org.

Also in the FOCUSed15 series

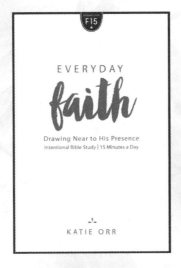

ISBN-13: 978-1-59669-461-3
N164101 · $11.99

What does real faith look like?

Everyday Faith, an easy-to-use, four-week study, helps you find out how to draw near to God's presence in as few as 15 minutes, five days a week. Designed for women who are pressed for time but crave depth from their Bible study, *Everyday Faith* utilizes the FOCUSed15 method, which values quality above quantity.

As it guides you through the Book of Hebrews, you will discover truths, promises, and commands; uncover word meanings; and discover your part in God's plan.

For more information, visit NewHopePublishers.com
and preview a video of Katie as she walks readers through
the FOCUS study method!

Also in the FOCUSed15 series

ISBN-13: 978-1-59669-462-0
N164102 · $11.99

Everyday Hope—an easy-to-use, four-week study—will help you discover how to hold fast to God's promises amidst feelings of hopelessness in as few as 15 minutes per day. Exploring the Scripture, you'll learn more about His promises as they apply to you now and in the days to come.

Designed for women who are pressed for time but crave depth from their Bible study, *Everyday Hope* offers a relevant and lasting approach for reading and understanding Scripture as you work through the FOCUS method each week:

F — Foundation:Enjoy every word
O — Observation: Look at the Details
C — Clarification: Uncover the Original Meaning
U — Utilization: Discover the Connections
S — Summation: Respond to God's Word

Make each minute of your valuable time count as you learn about His promises so you can hold fast to Him in the chaos of life.

For more information, visit NewHopePublishers.com
and preview a video of Katie as she walks readers
through the FOCUS study method!

WorldCrafts^{SM} develops sustainable,
fair-trade businesses among impoverished
people around the world.

Each WorldCrafts product represents lives changed
by the opportunity to earn an income with
dignity and to hear the offer of everlasting life.

Visit NewHopePublishers.com/FOCUSed15
to shop WorldCrafts products related to the
FOCUSed15 Bible study series!

WORLDCRAFTS^{SM}
Committed. Holistic. Fair Trade.
WorldCrafts.org 1-800-968-7301

WorldCrafts is a division of WMU®.